PASTA MENUS

PASTA MENUS

NORMAN KOLPAS

CB

CONTEMPORARY BOOKS

CHICAGO

Library of Congress Cataloging-in-Publication Data

Kolpas, Norman.
    Pasta menus : 52 easy, delicious, complete meals / Norman Kolpas.
      p.   cm.
    ISBN 0-8092-3914-0 (paper)
    1. Cookery (Pasta)   2. Menus.   I. Title.
TX809.M17K65   1993
641.8'22—dc20

92-39914
CIP

Published by Contemporary Books, Inc.
180 North Michigan Avenue, Chicago, Illinois 60601
Manufactured in the United States of America
International Standard Book Number: 0-8092-3914-0

CONTENTS

....

ACKNOWLEDGMENTS

·················

My heartfelt thanks go to my editor, Nancy Crossman, for suggesting that I write this book, and to all her colleagues at Contemporary Books who participated in its creation, including Kathy Willhoite, Cyndy Raucci, Georgene Sainati, Gigi Grajdura, Gerilee Hundt, Terry Stone, Ellen Kollmon, and Leah Mayes. Two of my Los Angeles–based colleagues—food photographer Brian Leatart and food stylist Norman Stewart—also deserve kudos for creating the beautiful cover photograph.

Among my taste testers, the most stalwart of all were my wife, Katie, and our son, Jacob. They are both a pleasure to cook for and the best companions I know for sharing a meal.

PASTA MENUS

1

INTRODUCTION

· · · · · · · · · · · · · · · · ·

Pasta is a proven favorite for any food lover seeking a main course that is easy to make, flavorful, and nutritious. But time and again, home cooks who have read and used my two previous books on pasta sauces—*Pasta Presto* and *Pasta Light*—have asked me for further information and advice to help them plan a full, satisfying, well-composed meal around pasta. What would be a good first course to serve before that sauce? What should I offer for dessert after it?

This book aims to answer such questions with 52 complete three-course menus featuring pasta as the main course. Each menu includes some simple hints on how to serve it, along with basic wine suggestions and some easy-to-follow guidelines on streamlining the meal's preparation.

To help you choose the right menu for any occasion, the menus are organized thematically into six chapters: those that are quickly prepared at the last minute; elegant menus for special occasions; robust meals; pasta menus with an emphasis on light yet satisfying ingredients and preparations; those ideal for casual occasions; and lunchtime pasta menus.

These categories are really only convenient slots into which I've organized the menus. When using this book, feel free to select any menu that appeals to you from any chapter, whatever the occasion might be. Don't hesitate to mix and match dishes from different menus.

A NOTE ON MENU YIELDS AND SERVING SIZES

For the sake of consistency and interchangeability of recipes, all the menus in this book are intended for four people, and the recipes within each menu consistently provide four good servings.

That yield has been specifically chosen to allow for easy adaptation to serving more or fewer people. Multiply the ingredients quantities by one and a half for six servings; double them to serve eight; halve them for two; and so on.

ELABORATING WITH BREAD, SALADS, AND PARMESAN
To avoid repetition, I've left out of the individual menus—with the exception of a few special recipes—any mention of two natural accompaniments to any pasta meal: good bread to dunk in the pasta sauce, and a crisp, green, refreshing side salad.

By all means, include them in any pasta menu you plan. Everywhere today, good little boutique bakeries are springing up offering wonderful breads in a variety of shapes and flavors. Seek them out, and select loaves that seem appropriate to the menu you are planning. And a wide range of salad leaves are now commonly available in supermarkets and greengroceries, ready to bring vivid tastes, colors, textures, and shapes to your salad bowl.

Nor should you hesitate to include Parmesan in your menu planning. Good block Parmesan—freshly grated and packaged at your market or deli, or grated by you at table—adds extra flavor to virtually any pasta dish.

A GUIDE TO PASTA

One of the benefits derived from the public's growing culinary awareness and sophistication in recent years is the wide range of pastas now on sale in supermarkets and gourmet shops everywhere. That range encompasses more than the myriad dried strands, ribbons, and shapes that have evolved in Italy over the centuries and found their way to these shores. It also embraces the many kinds of fresh pasta now commonly available—not merely made from egg-and-flour doughs but also flavored and colored with anything from tomatoes to squid ink, from spinach to saffron, to garlic and herbs. So popular have such flavored pastas become that they, in turn, are now being dried and sold in packaged form, extending the home larder's repertoire.

Don't let that range of choices confuse you. The principles of selecting what kind of pasta to serve remain fairly simple and logical. Generally, lighter sauces are best accompanied by more delicate pasta strands, while thicker sauces do better with broader ribbons to cling to. Thick, chunky sauces pair best with shells, tubes, or other shapes that match their consistency. When it comes to flavored pastas, let your own sense of what tastes good tell you what sauces will go well with them.

PASTA VARIETIES

The following fairly common pasta choices are grouped roughly by shape, to help you in your selection of the right pasta to serve with any menu. Feel free to substitute other pastas in the same category for those suggested in individual recipe introductions.

Strands

Angel Hair. Extra-fine strands. In Italian, *capelli d'angelo.*

Bavette. Slightly flattened spaghetti, oval in cross section.

Bucatini. Long, thin, spaghettilike tubes.

Fedelini. Very thin spaghetti.

Fusilli. "Fuses." Thin, squiggly strands as thick as spaghetti. (Also sometimes used to describe bite-sized pasta shapes.)

Perciatelli. Long, thin tubes about twice the thickness of spaghetti.

Spaghetti. The most familiar, most widely available stringlike pasta strands.

Vermicelli. "Little worms." Very thin spaghetti.

Ribbons

Fettucine. Long ribbons about ¼ inch in diameter. Sold either straight and flat or wound into small nests.

Fettuccelli. A narrower form of fettucine.

Fettucci. Ribbons about ½ inch wide.

Linguine. Very narrow, thick ribbons resembling flattened spaghetti.

Mafalde. Wide ribbons with rippled edges.

Papardelle. Wide, short ribbons.

Tagliarini. Small, thin tagliatelli.

Tagliatelli. Similar to fettuccine, but usually somewhat wider.

Shapes

Bocconcini. Grooved tubes about 1½ inches long and ½ inch in diameter.

Bow Ties. Shaped exactly like bow ties; available in varied sizes. Sometimes referred to as *farfalle.*

Cannolicchi. Small, ridged tubes.

Cavatelli. Narrow shells with rippled surfaces.

Conchiglie. Conch-shell shapes, varying in size and sometimes with grooved surfaces.

Ditali. Short macaroni tubes.

Farfalle. "Butterflies." Shapes similar to bow ties.

Fusilli. "Fuses." Short, corkscrew-shaped, or spiral pastas. (Sometimes refers to rotelli or to squiggly pasta strands.)

Gemelli. "Twins." Two short strands twined together.

Lumachi. Small, snail-shaped shells.

Macaroni. In general, any tubular pasta with a hole through the center. In practice, the term most often refers to *elbow* macaroni—small- to medium-sized, short, curved tubes.

Maruzze. Shells, varying from small to very large, sometimes smooth-surfaced and sometimes ridged.

Mostaccioli. "Little moustaches." Medium tubes, about 2 inches long, with diagonally cut ends. Sometimes with grooved surfaces. Often interchangeable with the narrower penne.

Orzo. Small, rice-shaped pasta.

Penne. "Pens." Short, narrow tubes with ends cut diagonally like a quill pen. Sometimes with grooved surfaces.

Rigatoni. Large, ridge-surfaced tubes.

4

Risi. Rice-shaped pasta, similar to orzo.

Rotini. Corkscrewlike spirals.

Ruote. Wagon wheel shapes.

Rotelli. Corkscrewlike spirals.

Spirali. Another term for fusilli or rotini.

Ziti. Long or short macaronilike tubes.

Filled Pastas and Miscellaneous

Agnolotti. Small, turnover-shaped semicircles.

Cannelloni. Large tubes for stuffing.

Cappelletti. Little stuffed hat shapes.

Gnocchi. Small hand-shaped dumplings, homemade or store-bought.

Lasagna. Long ribbons 2 to 3 inches wide, often with rippled edges; usually layered with filling, cheese, and sauces and then baked.

Manicotti. Large tubes for stuffing.

Ravioli. Familiar stuffed pasta squares.

Tortellini. Small stuffed crescent shapes closed into a circle.

COOKING PASTA

When cooking dried pasta, follow the manufacturer's package directions for best results. Here are some simple guidelines:

• Use a large quantity of water relative to the amount of pasta you are cooking, allowing plenty of room for the pasta to move around as it boils.

• Salt added to the water very lightly seasons the pasta. But leave it out if you're cutting down on salt.

• To test for doneness near the end of the cooking time, fish out a strand or piece of pasta with a long fork or slotted spoon. The pasta should be *al dente,* as the Italians describe it—cooked through but still slightly chewy.

• Drain the cooked pasta thoroughly, but do not rinse it. Sauce and serve it immediately.

A GUIDE TO BASIC INGREDIENTS

Butter. Recipes in this book call only for unsalted (sweet) butter, which has a fresher, purer flavor than salted butter and allows the home cook more leeway in seasoning any dish to taste. Buy it in quantity and keep extra sticks in the freezer.

Garlic. Buy whole heads and store them in a dry, airy place. To peel a garlic clove, separate it from the head and place it on the work surface. Place the side of a broad-bladed knife on top and hit down firmly—but not too hard—to crush the clove slightly. The skin will then slip off easily, leaving the clove ready to chop or to squeeze through a garlic press.

Herbs. Keep all dried herbs in airtight jars, stored away from light in a cool, dry place. Most supermarkets now carry a wide selection of fresh herbs; if fresh is unavailable, substitute the dried herb in about half the quantity.

Oil. Rich, fruity olive oil adds distinctive character to many pasta sauces, salad dressings, and other recipes. Choose only products labeled "extra-virgin" olive oil, extracted from the fruit on the first pressing without use of heat or chemicals. Among these, you'll find great variety, with different oils ranging in color from pale golden to dark green and corresponding in taste from mild to strongly olive-flavored. Buy small quantities, sample, and compare until you find one or more that suit your personal taste.

Store olive oil in its airtight container, away from heat and light.

Tomatoes and Tomato Paste. When vine-ripened tomatoes are available at the height of summer, jump at the chance to use them; at other times of year, when fresh tomatoes are called for, Roma tomatoes are the best choice.

When using canned tomatoes, avoid preseasoned kinds, opting for plain, peeled tomatoes—whether whole, crushed, or chopped—in their natural juices. Many different brands are commonly available on supermarket shelves, in both 16-ounce and 28-ounce sizes; experiment with a few and arrive at a brand that tastes best to you.

The same advice holds true for tomato pastes. One product worth seeking out, however, is Italian double-strength tomato concentrate, twice as strong as conventional canned tomato paste and with an excellent tomato flavor. If you can find it (the brand I use is called Amore, imported by Liberty-Richter, Inc., Carlstadt, NJ 07072), use half the quantity of ordinary tomato paste called for in the recipe.

BASIC RECIPES AND PREPARATIONS

These few simple recipes and preparations are called for and cross-referenced throughout the book.

BALSAMIC VINAIGRETTE

The intense flavor of well-aged balsamic vinegar adds a marvelous richness to this simple dressing. Substitute good red-wine or sherry vinegar, if you like, and elaborate the dressing with a teaspoon of mustard or some fresh or dried herbs stirred into the vinegar with the other seasonings.

> *¼ cup balsamic vinegar*
> *¼ teaspoon salt*
> *¼ teaspoon white pepper*
> *¾ cup olive oil*

In a mixing bowl, stir together the vinegar, salt, and pepper until the salt dissolves. Stirring briskly, slowly pour in the olive oil.

LEMON VINAIGRETTE

Use this dressing when you want a lighter, slightly sweeter taste than you'd get from a vinegar-based vinaigrette. Feel free to enhance the dressing with fresh or dried herbs or mustard stirred into the lemon juice with the other seasonings.

> ¼ cup fresh lemon juice
> ½ teaspoon salt
> ¼ teaspoon sugar
> ¼ teaspoon white pepper
> ¾ cup olive oil

In a mixing bowl, stir together the lemon juice, salt, sugar, and pepper until the salt and sugar dissolve. Stirring briskly, slowly pour in the olive oil.

ROASTING BELL PEPPERS

To roast peppers, place them on a baking sheet in a 500°F oven. Roast until the skins are evenly blistered and browned, about 25 minutes, carefully turning the peppers two or three times so they roast evenly. Remove them from the oven and cover with a kitchen towel.

When the peppers are cool enough to handle, pull out the stems, peel away the blackened skins, tear open the peppers, and remove the seeds, using a teaspoon to pick up any strays.

PEELING AND SEEDING TOMATOES

Some sauces benefit from the removal of tomatoes' shiny skins and watery, tasteless seed sacs. To peel fresh tomatoes, first bring a large saucepan of water to a boil. With a small, sharp knife, remove the core of each tomato and lightly score its skin in four segments. Carefully put the tomatoes into the water and parboil for about 30 seconds; then lift them out with a slotted spoon. When the tomatoes are cool enough to handle, peel off their skins.

To seed the tomatoes, cut them in half horizontally. With your finger or the handle of a teaspoon, gently scoop out the seed sacs and discard them.

2
PASTA MEALS IN AN INSTANT

·················

CELEBRATION OF SPRING

Serves 4

Simple Salad of Baby Greens
Pasta Primavera Sauté
Early Berries with Fruit Liqueurs and Mint

When the weather begins to warm up and the markets start showing off the freshest, tenderest vegetables and fruits, celebrate the season with this quickly prepared, light yet satisfying menu. Bright white china or sparkling glass plates best show off the springtime colors. Accompany the meal with a crisp white wine.

Wash the salad greens an hour or two before dinner and have them wrapped in a damp kitchen towel, crisping in the refrigerator. For the main course, cut up all the vegetables in advance so they'll be ready to sauté while the pasta cooks. The berries just need a fast picking over and a quick rinse about half an hour before mealtime; leave them in the strainer in the sink after rinsing, so excess moisture can drip away.

SIMPLE SALAD OF BABY GREENS

The growing interest in fresh, top-quality ingredients has brought an outstanding selection of fresh new produce to our markets, not least of which is the selection of tiny, tender-crisp baby salad greens—from butter lettuce to oak leaf and red leaf, endive to radicchio to chicory. In fact, many markets sell a medley of baby greens already tossed, bagged, and ready to use. If yours doesn't sell baby greens, just use the smallest, freshest ones you can find.

> *8 cups baby salad greens*
> *Lemon Vinaigrette (page 8)*
> *3–4 ounces blue cheese, crumbled*
>   *(optional)*

Just before serving, put the greens in a large salad bowl or mixing bowl and toss with just enough of the vinaigrette to coat them lightly. Serve on chilled salad plates, garnishing if you like with a little crumbled blue cheese.

PASTA PRIMAVERA SAUTE

In this rapid sauté of fresh springtime vegetables, feel free to substitute your favorites and vary the mix of ingredients based on the best the season offers. Use bite-sized pasta shapes about the same size as the vegetable pieces, such as penne, fusilli, rotini, rigatoni, radiatori, or medium-sized shells.

¾ pound uncooked pasta
¾ cup olive oil
2 medium cloves garlic, finely
   chopped
1 cup small- to medium-sized
   broccoli florets
1 cup 1-by-¼-inch strips carrot
1 cup 1-by-¼-inch strips zucchini
1 cup small snow peapods, trimmed
1 cup thinly sliced button
   mushrooms

1 cup thinly sliced red, yellow, or
   green bell pepper
½ cup grated Parmesan
¼ cup finely chopped fresh Italian
   parsley
¼ cup finely shredded fresh basil
   leaves
Freshly ground black pepper

Bring a large pot of salted water to a boil and add the pasta; cook until al dente, following package directions.

When the pasta is about halfway done cooking, prepare the vegetables. In a large skillet or wok, heat the olive oil over moderate-to-high heat. Add the garlic; as soon as it sizzles, add all the vegetables and sauté, stirring constantly, until they are tender-crisp, 3 to 5 minutes.

In a mixing bowl, toss the vegetables and oil with the cooked and drained pasta. Add the Parmesan, parsley, basil, and plenty of black pepper to taste and toss again. Serve immediately.

EARLY BERRIES WITH FRUIT LIQUEURS AND MINT

Modern air freight has made it possible to get pretty good berries year-round. But watch for the earliest berries of the season to serve as a simple, no-fuss dessert; offer one kind or a mixture of two or more, depending on what's available and in peak condition. To highlight their tastes, offer your guests a selection of fruit liqueurs or brandies such as cherry-flavored kirsch, raspberry framboise, or orange curaçao.

2–3 pints assorted berries
Fresh mint sprigs, for garnish
Assorted fruit liqueurs

Just before serving, arrange the berries in individual chilled serving dishes, garnishing them with mint sprigs. Present one or more fruit liqueurs with them at table, letting each guest drizzle a little liqueur to taste over his or her serving.

ARRIVEDERCI ROMA

Serves 4

Seasonal Melon with Prosciutto
Classic Fettucine Alfredo
Assorted Fruit Gellati and Biscotti

The time you spend preparing a meal matters nowhere near as much as the care you've shown in selecting what you offer—as this menu stylishly proves. Serve it on your best china, the better to highlight the quality of the ingredients. And offer white or blush wine in your best crystal.

The appetizer and dessert require only a quick stop at a good supermarket or Italian delicatessen. The main course is a last-minute preparation—in fact, if you want to be particularly stylish, you can even make it in a chafing dish at table, just as they do at the Roman restaurant that invented it.

SEASONAL MELON WITH PROSCIUTTO

The sweet perfume of a ripe melon finds a perfect counterpoint in the intense, salty-sweet tang of the famous cured raw ham of Parma, Italy. Be sure to ask the deli to slice the prosciutto as thinly as possible: it should be translucent.

> *1 large ripe honeydew, cantaloupe, or*
>   *Cranshaw melon*
> *3 ounces prosciutto, sliced paper-thin*
> *1 tablespoon finely chopped fresh*
>   *Italian parsley*

About 30 minutes before serving, cut the melon into quarters, scoop out and discard the seeds, and peel away the rinds. Cut each quarter into 3 thin wedges and arrange on individual serving plates. Drape the prosciutto over the melon and garnish with parsley.

CLASSIC FETTUCINE ALFREDO

No cooked sauce could be faster or taste more lavish than this specialty of Rome's Alfredo alla Scrofa restaurant. Use fresh or dried fettucine pasta, or other ribbons such as tagliatelli or linguine.

> ¾ pound uncooked pasta
> 1½ cups heavy cream
> ½ cup (1 stick) unsalted butter, cut
>   into pieces
> 1½ cups grated Parmesan
> Dash nutmeg (optional)
> 2 tablespoons finely chopped fresh
>   chives or Italian parsley
> Freshly ground black pepper

Bring a large pot of salted water to a boil and add the pasta; cook until al dente, following package directions.

Just a few minutes before the pasta is done, heat the cream and butter together in a medium saucepan over medium heat, stirring occasionally, until the butter melts and the cream is hot.

Gradually stir in 1 cup of Parmesan and, if you like, the nutmeg. As soon as the cheese has melted and the pasta is done, drain the cooked pasta thoroughly and add it to the sauce. Stir and gently toss to coat the pasta evenly. Transfer to individual serving plates and garnish with chives or parsley. Pass extra Parmesan and black pepper for guests to add generously to taste.

ASSORTED FRUIT GELLATI AND BISCOTTI

Check the freezer case of your best local market or Italian delicatessen for a selection of fresh-fruit Italian-style gellati or sorbets, selecting at least two different pints to offer your guests. While you're there, buy two or three different varieties of packaged or fresh-baked Italian biscotti—crisp cookies in varied shapes, embellished with nuts, fruits, spices, or chocolate—to pass on a plate alongside. Offer strong black coffee or fresh-brewed espresso, too.

SUMMERTIME FLAVORS

Serves 4

Tricolor Salad with Anchovies
Pasta with Tuna, Red Onions, and Parmesan Shavings
Brandied Peach–Vanilla Sundaes

This easy menu offers sprightly flavors to spark the appetite at the end of a sluggish summer day. Serve it on casual, everyday plates and accompany with a crisp white wine, sparkling wine, spritzers, or beer.

The salad is quickly assembled in advance, and the pasta is prepared in a few brief moments before serving time. For the dessert, peel and slice the peaches ahead of time so they'll be ready to warm quickly as an elegant ice cream topping.

TRICOLOR SALAD WITH ANCHOVIES

The classic tricolor combination of mozzarella, tomatoes, and basil gets the added embellishment of anchovy fillets in this quickly assembled salad. If you can find it, use fresh buffalo-milk mozzarella.

> 6 large Roma tomatoes, cored and
>   cut into ¼-inch-thick slices
> ½ pound mozzarella, thinly sliced
> 8–12 drained canned anchovy fillets
> Lemon Vinaigrette (page 8)
> 6 tablespoons thinly shredded fresh
>   basil
> Freshly ground black pepper

About 30 minutes before serving, arrange the tomato and cheese slices in an overlapping pattern on individual serving plates or a serving platter. Drape the anchovies on top. Cover and refrigerate.

Just before serving, drizzle the vinaigrette over the salad. Sprinkle with shredded basil and add freshly ground black pepper to taste.

PASTA WITH TUNA, RED ONIONS,
AND PARMESAN SHAVINGS

Use good-quality tuna—preferably the Italian variety packed in olive oil—for this fast, simple dish. This is particularly attractive with bow tie–shaped pasta or other bite-sized shapes.

¾ pound uncooked pasta
¾ cup olive oil
1 large red onion, thinly sliced
¼ cup finely chopped Italian parsley
2 6½-ounce cans tuna in oil,
    drained and broken into coarse
    chunks
6 ounces block Parmesan, cut into
    wide, thin shavings with a
    vegetable peeler
1 lemon, halved
Freshly ground black pepper

Bring a large pot of salted water to a boil and add the pasta; cook until al dente, following package directions.

In a large skillet, heat the oil over moderate heat. Add the onion and sauté just until it begins to turn translucent, 1 to 2 minutes.

As soon as the pasta is done, drain well and toss in a serving bowl with the onions and oil and the parsley. Transfer to serving plates and scatter tuna chunks and Parmesan on top. Squeeze lemon juice over each portion and season generously with black pepper.

BRANDIED PEACH-VANILLA SUNDAES

The brandy, its alcohol flambéed away at serving time, adds an extra-lavish touch to this simply prepared dessert.

>1 quart vanilla ice cream
>¼ cup brandy
>4 tablespoons unsalted butter
>2 large ripe peaches, peeled, pitted,
>   and thinly sliced, or 2 cups frozen
>   peaches
>2 tablespoons sugar
>½ teaspoon ground cinnamon

In advance, scoop the ice cream into 4 temperature-resistant serving dishes and put them in the freezer.

A few minutes before serving, put the brandy to warm in a small bowl set inside a larger bowl of hot water.

In a saucepan, melt the butter over medium heat. Add the peaches, sugar, and cinnamon and sauté, stirring gently, just until heated through, 2 to 3 minutes.

Spoon the hot peaches over the individual servings of ice cream and, the moment before presenting them, carefully spoon the warmed brandy on top and use a long wooden match to ignite the brandy.

SIMPLE TASTES

Serves 4

Butter Lettuce, Cucumber, and Bay Shrimp Salad
Spaghetti with Browned Butter, Garlic, and Bread Crumbs
Lemon Sorbet with Raspberry Sauce

Though simple in preparation and fairly light on the stomach, this menu is strong on flair and flavor. Darker-colored plates, if you have them, will contrast beautifully with the pale colors and simple presentation of the food. Accompany with a robust white or light red wine.

Thanks to the precooked bay shrimp sold by most good fishmongers and in supermarket seafood departments, the salads are assembled in but a moment. The main course takes no longer than the cooking time of the pasta itself. Pre-purchased lemon sorbet is embellished with a quickly pureed sauce made in advance from fresh or frozen raspberries; together, they nicely cleanse the palate after the garlicky pasta.

BUTTER LETTUCE, CUCUMBER, AND BAY SHRIMP SALAD

Fresh and light though it is on the palate, this salad is wonderfully satisfying.

> 6 cups butter lettuce leaves, left
> whole if small, torn into bite-sized
> pieces if larger
> 1 medium cucumber, peeled, halved
> lengthwise, seeded, and thinly
> sliced
> 1 pound precooked bay shrimp
> Lemon Vinaigrette (page 8)
> 2 tablespoons finely chopped fresh
> dill, or 1 tablespoon dried dill
> Fresh dill or parsley sprigs, for
> garnish

Arrange the lettuce leaves in an attractive pattern on individual serving plates. Arrange a bed of sliced cucumber in the center of each arrangement and mound the shrimp on top.

In a small bowl, stir together the vinaigrette and the chopped dill. Just before serving, drizzle the dressing generously over the shrimp, cucumber, and lettuce. Garnish with the dill or parsley sprigs.

SPAGHETTI WITH BROWNED BUTTER, GARLIC, AND BREAD CRUMBS

A fine example of the principle that the whole is often greater than the sum of the parts. Browned in butter, the garlic and bread crumbs take on a rich, nutty flavor and crisp texture that wonderfully complements al dente pasta. Use spaghetti, linguine, or other regular-sized strands.

¾ pound uncooked pasta
½ cup (1 stick) unsalted butter, cut
   into pieces
¼ cup olive oil
3 medium cloves garlic, finely
   chopped
1 cup fine fresh bread crumbs
¼ cup finely chopped fresh Italian
   parsley
Salt and freshly ground black pepper
½ cup fresh grated Parmesan

Bring a large pot of salted water to a boil and add the pasta; cook until al dente, following package directions.

A few minutes before the pasta is done, melt the butter with the oil in a medium skillet over moderate heat. When the butter begins to foam, add the garlic and sauté about 30 seconds. Add the bread crumbs and continue sautéing, stirring constantly, until the mixture turns golden brown, 3 to 4 minutes. Stir in the parsley.

Add the cooked and drained pasta to the skillet and toss to mix well with the bread crumbs. Season to taste with salt and pepper. Serve immediately, passing Parmesan on the side.

LEMON SORBET WITH RASPBERRY SAUCE

Check your market's freezer case for the best quality lemon sorbet you can find. The quickly prepared sauce contrasts brilliantly in both color and flavor.

RASPBERRY SAUCE
1½ cups fresh or defrosted frozen
    raspberries, ¼ cup reserved
⅓ cup sugar

1½ pints lemon sorbet
Fresh mint sprigs, for garnish

For the sauce, put 1¼ cups of the raspberries with the sugar in a food processor or blender and puree. Pour the puree into a sieve set over a mixing bowl and press it through with a spatula or wooden spoon. Discard the seeds. Cover the bowl and refrigerate until serving time.

Scoop the sorbet into individual chilled serving bowls or dishes. Drizzle the raspberry sauce on top and garnish with the reserved berries and mint sprigs.

ROBUST WINTER REPAST

Serves 4

Garlic-Herb Loaf
Pasta with Ground Beef, Sizzled Onions, and Cheddar
Baked Apples with Walnuts and Raisins

This is hearty, satisfying food for a cold evening, and its simple preparation lets you spend more time huddled around the fire. Serve it on comfortable old crockery, with coarse-woven linens. Beer or a robust red wine would make a good accompaniment.

Prepare the bread at least an hour in advance—ready to pop into the oven with the baked apples. As soon as they begin baking, start the pasta—which will be ready to eat at the same time the bread comes out of the oven.

GARLIC-HERB LOAF

½ cup (1 stick) unsalted butter,
*   softened*
1 tablespoon dried oregano
1 tablespoon finely chopped fresh
*   chives or freeze-dried chives*
1 tablespoon finely chopped fresh
*   Italian parsley*
2–3 cloves garlic, crushed
1 12- to 16-inch-long loaf Italian
*   bread*

Preheat the oven to 350°F.

In a mixing bowl, use a table fork to mash together the butter, herbs, and garlic until smoothly blended.

With a bread knife, cut the bread loaf lengthwise in half. Spread the butter mixture generously on the cut side of each half. Put the loaf back together, wrap securely in aluminum foil, and bake for about 30 minutes. Then unwrap and cut crosswise into generous slices.

PASTA WITH GROUND BEEF, SIZZLED ONIONS, AND CHEDDAR

A simple version of a skillet supper, this pasta dish combines the intense flavors of browned onions, browned beef, and sharp cheddar, tossed in the pan with cooked pasta. Use medium-sized elbow macaroni or other pasta shapes.

¾ pound uncooked pasta
2 tablespoons unsalted butter
2 tablespoons vegetable oil
3 medium onions, finely chopped
1 clove garlic, finely chopped
1 pound lean ground beef
1 cup beef broth
1 teaspoon dried thyme
1 teaspoon dried oregano
½ teaspoon salt
½ pound sharp cheddar, coarsely
   shredded
¼ cup finely chopped fresh Italian
   parsley

Bring a large pot of salted water to a boil and add the pasta; cook until al dente, following package directions.

As soon as the pasta starts cooking, melt the butter with the oil in a large skillet or saucepan over moderate-to-high heat. Add the onions and garlic and sauté until they begin to turn golden brown, 3 to 5 minutes. Add the beef and sauté, breaking it up coarsely with a wooden spoon, until it has lost all its pink color and begun to brown, about 10 minutes.

Add the broth, thyme, oregano, and salt; stir and scrape to deglaze the pan deposits. Bring to a boil and continue boiling briskly until the broth has reduced to a thick, saucelike consistency, 5 to 7 minutes. Reduce the heat, add the cooked and drained pasta, cheddar, and parsley, and toss well until the cheese begins to melt. Serve immediately.

BAKED APPLES WITH WALNUTS AND RAISINS

Add a scoop of whipped cream or vanilla ice cream to each serving, if you like.

> *4 large cooking apples, cored, skins*
> *scored with a knife*
> *⅓ cup coarsely chopped walnuts*
> *⅓ cup seedless golden or brown*
> *raisins*
> *1 cup water*
> *½ cup brown sugar*
> *2 tablespoons unsalted butter*
> *1 teaspoon ground cinnamon*
> *1 teaspoon grated orange zest*

Preheat the oven to 350°F.

Put the apples in a baking dish just large enough to hold them. In a small bowl, toss together the walnuts and raisins and spoon the mixture into the center of each apple.

In a small saucepan, stir together the water and sugar. Bring to a boil over moderate heat, reduce the heat slightly, and simmer about 2 minutes more. Stir in the butter, cinnamon, and orange zest.

Drizzle the syrup over and around the apples and into their centers. Bake until the apples are tender, about 1 hour, basting 3 or 4 times. Serve hot or lukewarm.

TRATTORIA FAVORITES

Serves 4

Chopped Salad
Linguine with White Clam Sauce
Simple Spumoni

Put these popular restaurant dishes together in moments at home and create the illusion that you're dining in your favorite trattoria. To enhance the illusion, set the table with sturdy white crockery and red-checked linens—not to mention a candle stuck in a wine bottle. Speaking of wine, a sturdy white or light Italian red such as Chianti would do fine.

The spumoni, though it takes only a minute or two of actual work, requires preparation a few hours in advance to allow the ice cream time to refreeze. But the salad and the clam sauce are easily prepared just before serving.

CHOPPED SALAD

When you're pressed for time, the beauty of a classic Italian chopped salad is that you don't have to fuss with presentation. Just chop all the ingredients, toss them together, and dress them. Feel free to vary the kinds of meats and cheeses you add.

4 cups coarsely chopped iceberg
   lettuce
½ cup finely chopped red onion
½ cup canned, drained garbanzo
   beans, coarsely chopped
½ cup pitted black olives, coarsely
   chopped
6 ounces thinly sliced Italian-style
   salami, coarsely chopped
6 ounces thinly sliced provolone
   cheese, coarsely chopped
4 firm, ripe Roma tomatoes, cored,
   halved, seeded, and coarsely
   chopped
Balsamic Vinaigrette (page 7)
¼ cup finely chopped fresh parsley
8 Italian pickled pepperoncini,
   drained (optional)

In a mixing bowl, thoroughly toss together the lettuce, onion, garbanzos, olives, salami, provolone, and tomatoes. Add enough dressing to coat generously and toss well. Spoon onto chilled serving plates and garnish with parsley and pepperoncini, if desired.

LINGUINE WITH WHITE CLAM SAUCE

Canned baby clams and bottled clam juice, both widely available, make this pasta dish a cinch to prepare. In place of linguine, you can use spaghetti or tagliarini.

> ¾ pound uncooked pasta
> 2 tablespoons unsalted butter
> 6 tablespoons olive oil
> 4 cloves garlic, finely chopped
> 3 10¼-ounce cans whole baby clams,
>   drained
> ¼ cup finely chopped fresh parsley
> 1 cup bottled clam juice
> 3 tablespoons fresh lemon juice
> 1 tablespoon dried basil
> 1 tablespoon dried oregano
> ½ teaspoon salt
> ½ teaspoon freshly ground black
>   pepper

Bring a large pot of salted water to a boil and add the pasta; cook until al dente, following package directions.

In a large skillet, melt the butter with the oil over moderate heat. Add the garlic and sauté until it just begins to turn golden, 3 to 4 minutes.

Add the clams and parsley; sauté for 1 minute more. Then add the remaining ingredients and simmer gently for about 3 minutes.

Drain the pasta and place in individual serving bowls. Pour the sauce over the pasta.

SIMPLE SPUMONI

If you can't hunt down a commercial version of the favorite trattoria ice cream, make this reasonable facsimile yourself.

> 1½ *pints vanilla ice cream, softened*
> ¼ *cup marsala*
> ⅓ *cup assorted candied fruits,*
>   *coarsely chopped*
> ⅓ *cup coarsely chopped almonds or*
>   *walnuts*
> ⅓ *cup semisweet chocolate chips*
>   *(optional)*

Leave the ice cream at room temperature until soft, about 30 minutes. Transfer it to a mixing bowl and stir in the marsala until blended. Then fold in the fruits, nuts, and, if you like, chocolate chips. Return the ice cream to its carton and freeze for at least 1 hour.

LAST-MINUTE SUPPER

Serves 4

Tapenade Toasts
Pasta with Fresh Tomato Filet
Fresh Fruit and Cheese Platter

Are last-minute guests about to land on your doorstep? A quick stop at the market can yield the makings of this simple yet celebratory feast—which you can elaborate further with a salad of your choice. Break out the best china, to make it look like anything but a spur-of-the-moment occasion. Your favorite sparkling wine could be served first course to last.

The tapenade requires just rapid pureeing in a food processor. Set out the appetizer with drinks for guests while you duck into the kitchen to quickly assemble the pasta.

TAPENADE TOASTS

The simple olive-and-anchovy spread of southern France will dazzle even more if you serve it on a really outstanding bread from your best local bakery. It's especially good on sourdough or toasted walnut bread.

> 1 small loaf freshly baked bread,
>   thinly sliced, slices cut into
>   quarters
> 1½ cups Mediterranean-style black
>   olives, pitted
> ½ cup olive oil
> ¼ cup packed fresh parsley
> 2 tablespoons drained capers
> 2 tablespoons fresh lemon juice
> 1 tablespoon cognac or brandy
> 1 large clove garlic
> 1 2-ounce tin anchovy fillets,
>   drained

Preheat the broiler. Arrange the bread slices in a single layer on a baking sheet and broil until golden brown, 1 to 2 minutes per side, taking care that they do not burn.

Then, put the remaining ingredients in a food processor fitted with a metal blade. Turning the machine on and off rapidly, pulse the ingredients several times until coarsely chopped. Scrape down the work bowl. Then process continuously until smooth.

Spread the toasts with the puree. Or serve the tapenade in a bowl on a platter, surrounded by the toasts, with knives for guests to spread it themselves onto the toasts.

PASTA WITH FRESH TOMATO FILET

Year-round, plum-shaped Roma tomatoes are the best choice for this quick sauce that highlights their fresh flavor. Serve with angel hair, spaghettini, or other fine strands.

1½ pounds Roma tomatoes
¾ pound uncooked pasta
¼ cup olive oil
2 medium cloves garlic, finely
    chopped
¼ cup packed finely shredded fresh
    basil leaves, or 2 tablespoons
    dried basil
½ teaspoon salt
1 teaspoon sugar (optional)

Bring 2 large saucepans of salted water to a boil. With a small, sharp knife, remove the core of each tomato and lightly score its skin into four segments. Put the tomatoes in the water and parboil about 30 seconds; then lift them out with a slotted spoon or wire skimmer and dip into a bowl of cold water.

Peel off the tomatoes' skins. Cut each in half horizontally and, with your finger or the handle of a teaspoon, scoop out and discard the seeds. Coarsely chop the tomato pulp.

Put the pasta into the other pot of boiling water; cook until al dente, following package directions.

Meanwhile, in a large skillet, heat the olive oil over moderate heat. Add the garlic and sauté for about 1 minute. Add the tomatoes, raise the heat, and sauté them just until their juices thicken, about 5 minutes.

Add the herbs and salt; if the tomatoes are not peak-of-season and deep red in color, add the sugar, too. Simmer about 1 minute more. Pour over the cooked and drained pasta.

FRESH FRUIT AND CHEESE PLATTER

A platter of fresh seasonal fruits and creamy cheeses makes an especially attractive and tempting dessert offering at the end of a simple but elegant meal. Good pairings include pears and French Brie or Camembert; grapes and Italian fontina; or apples and English Stilton. Include a selection of crisp crackers on which guests can spread the cheese.

ASIAN EXPRESS

Serves 4

Egg Drop Soup
Easy Chow Mein–Style Pasta with Leftover Chicken
Lychees and Mandarin Oranges

Chinese cuisine remains one of our favorite forms of fast food—fresh, flavorful, and ready in almost an instant. The same principles apply when you cook Chinese food at home, as this menu tastily demonstrates. Serve on plain white everyday tableware or on the pretty but inexpensive dishes frequently found in Chinese shops. Accompany with a Chinese or Japanese lager.

While the menu is Asian, virtually all of the ingredients are commonly available in the West. Apart from cutting up the vegetables and shredding the chicken, virtually no advance preparation is necessary.

EGG DROP SOUP

That Chinese restaurant standby takes just a few seconds to prepare.

1½ quarts chicken broth
2 teaspoons light soy sauce
2 teaspoons cornstarch
2 eggs
1 tablespoon finely chopped fresh
  parsley

Set aside ¼ cup of the chicken broth. In a medium saucepan over moderate heat, bring the remaining chicken broth to a boil; reduce the heat to a bare simmer.

Meanwhile, put the soy sauce in a small bowl and stir in the cornstarch until completely dissolved. In a separate bowl, lightly beat the eggs and whisk in the reserved broth.

Stir the soy sauce–cornstarch mixture into the soup. As soon as it begins to thicken, add the egg mixture and stir vigorously to break the egg up into thin wisps as it cooks. Serve immediately, garnished with parsley.

EASY CHOW MEIN-STYLE PASTA
WITH LEFTOVER CHICKEN

This is a great way to extend leftover roast chicken. Or use fresh raw chicken, adding the thinly sliced meat to the wok along with the onion, celery, and carrot. You can serve the sauce over any kind of medium-sized pasta strands or ribbons, such as spaghetti, linguine, fettucine, or tagliarini. But if your market or a nearby Asian shop carries dried or fresh Chinese egg noodles, by all means try it over them.

¾ pound uncooked pasta
¼ cup vegetable oil
¼ cup slivered almonds
1 medium clove garlic, finely
   chopped
½ tablespoon grated fresh ginger root
1 small onion, coarsely chopped
1 stalk celery, thinly sliced
1 small carrot, cut diagonally into ⅛-
   inch-thick slices
1 small red bell pepper, halved,
   stemmed, seeded, and cut into ¼-
   by 2-inch strips

2 ounces button mushrooms, cut
   into ¼-inch-thick slices
2 cups cooked leftover chicken meat,
   coarsely shredded
2 tablespoons light soy sauce
1 tablespoon Worcestershire sauce
1 cup chicken broth
1 tablespoon cornstarch
2 medium scallions, thinly sliced
2 tablespoons finely chopped fresh
   cilantro

Bring a large pot of salted water to a boil and add the pasta; cook until al dente, following package directions.

In a large wok or skillet, heat 2 tablespoons of the oil over high heat. Add the almonds and stir-fry just until they begin to turn golden, about 1 minute; remove with a slotted spoon and drain on paper towels. Add the remaining oil, garlic, and ginger and stir-fry 30 seconds to 1 minute; add the onion, celery, and carrot and stir-fry for 1 minute more. Then add the bell pepper and mushrooms and sauté another minute.

Add the chicken and toss well with the vegetables. Add the soy and Worcestershire sauces and stir and scrape briefly to deglaze. Add ¾ cup of the broth to the wok. Dissolve the cornstarch in the remaining broth and, as soon as the liquid in the wok simmers, stir in the cornstarch mixture. Continue simmering until the liquid thickens to coating consistency, 1 to 2 minutes. Spoon over the cooked and drained pasta and garnish with the almonds, scallions, and cilantro.

LYCHEES AND MANDARIN ORANGES

While both fruits are available fresh only rarely, they can be found dependably canned in Asian markets and the Asian food sections of well-stocked supermarkets. Buy a can of each and chill well in the refrigerator. If you can't find one of the fruits, substitute canned pineapple chunks. Serve together in individual bowls, garnished with fresh mint sprigs and enhanced, if you like, with a splash of Grand Marnier. Accompany with hot green tea.

CASUALLY IMPRESSIVE DINNER

Serves 4

Orange and Red Onion Salad
Pasta with Basil-Walnut Pesto
Vanilla Frozen Yogurt with Raspberry Swirl

Quickly prepared though this meal may be, it nevertheless dazzles with vibrant colors—the bright orange and red of the appetizer, the deep green of the pesto sauce, the neon red of the raspberry swirl—and tastes to match. Serve it on white or pale-colored tableware, or jet-black plates, to contrast with the vivid hues.

If you have time, prepare the salad an hour or so in advance, giving the flavors some time to mingle. The dessert, too, should be prepared ahead of time. Make the pesto just before you place the main course on the table.

ORANGE AND RED ONION SALAD

One of the most surprising little salads I know, this combination pleases the eye with its bright colors and delights the palate with its surprisingly subtle yet vibrant tastes.

>3 large navel oranges
>1 medium red onion, very thinly
>   sliced
>2 tablespoons finely chopped fresh
>   parsley
>2 tablespoons balsamic vinegar
>Freshly ground black pepper

Using a sharp knife, peel the oranges, slicing off the fruit segments' outer membranes along with the peel. With the knife, segment the oranges, cutting each segment out from its membranes and putting it in a mixing bowl. Add the onion and parsley, drizzle with balsamic vinegar, and toss gently. Cover and refrigerate until serving time. Just before serving, add black pepper to taste.

PASTA WITH BASIL-WALNUT PESTO

The popular Genovese fresh basil sauce becomes all the easier to make with a nut that's much more of a kitchen staple—and much easier to find in the markets— than the pine nuts that are traditionally used. A food processor purees the sauce instantly. Toss it with your favorite strands or ribbons, such as spaghetti, angel hair, linguine, or fettucine.

> ¾ pound uncooked pasta
> 3 cups packed stemmed fresh basil
>   leaves
> 1½ cups olive oil
> 1 cup grated Parmesan
> ⅔ cup shelled walnuts
> 3 medium cloves garlic

Bring a large pot of salted water to a boil and add the pasta; cook until al dente, following package directions.

Meanwhile, put all remaining ingredients in a food processor fitted with a metal blade. Turning the machine on and off rapidly, pulse the ingredients several times until coarsely chopped. Scrape down the work bowl, then process continuously until the sauce is smooth. If it seems too thick to coat the pasta, pulse in a little hot water.

As soon as the pasta is done, drain well and transfer to a serving bowl. Toss well with the sauce. Serve immediately.

VANILLA FROZEN YOGURT WITH RASPBERRY SWIRL

While frozen yogurt satisfies the urge for something creamy, its underlying tartness—complemented by the raspberry swirl—makes it an excellent palate-cleanser after a rich main course. The plethora of frozen yogurt shops—as well as commercial brands available in supermarkets—makes it as easy to find as ice cream. If you don't have the time to swirl in the raspberry sauce, pour it over scoops of the yogurt.

> *1½ pints good-quality vanilla frozen*
> *   yogurt*
> *Raspberry Sauce (see page 28)*

If you've purchased soft-serve frozen yogurt, as soon as you get it home prepare the Raspberry Sauce. Transfer the yogurt to a bowl, drizzle the sauce over it, and fold several times with a rubber spatula to swirl the sauce through the yogurt. Return it to its container and put it in the freezer until serving time.

If the yogurt you purchased is frozen hard, let it soften at room temperature for about 30 minutes while you prepare the sauce; then follow the above instructions.

To serve, scoop the yogurt into chilled dishes. Garnish with the reserved raspberries.

3

A TOUCH OF ELEGANCE

....

AFTER-THEATER SUPPER

Serves 4

Fresh Oysters with Cilantro Salsa
Angel Hair with Caviar and Chives
Lemon-Champagne Granita

This menu presents small but satisfying quantities of absolutely luxurious ingredients to make a light, memorable late-night supper. Serve it on your finest china. You can pour champagne or sparkling wine from first course to last.

The only advance work involved is preparing the granita, which can be made the night before.

FRESH OYSTERS WITH CILANTRO SALSA

Purists will understandably swear that they need only a squeeze of lemon to complement a fresh oyster. But, for the more adventurous of heart, a dab of fresh cilantro salsa makes a wonderful accompaniment to the briny creatures. Buy fresh oysters only from the best, most reputable seafood source you can find and as close to serving time as possible. If they smell anything less than absolutely fresh, with the clean, salty scent of sea air, do not buy them. If you aren't a dab hand at opening oysters, the fishmonger should be able to do it for you and pack them on the half shell on a bed of crushed ice.

¼ cup finely chopped fresh cilantro
3 tablespoons lime or fresh lemon
    juice
2 tablespoons olive oil
2 tablespoons finely chopped fresh
    chives
1 small mild green Anaheim chili,
    halved, stemmed, seeded, and
    finely chopped
Salt and freshly ground black pepper
2 dozen fresh oysters, well-scrubbed
    and opened, on the half shell
2 lemons, cut into wedges

In a mixing bowl, stir together the cilantro, lime or lemon juice, olive oil, chives, and chili; season to taste with salt and pepper. Cover with plastic wrap and refrigerate until serving time.

Arrange the oysters on a platter covered with crushed ice, or on individual soup plates filled with crushed ice. Pass the salsa and lemon wedges on the side.

ANGEL HAIR WITH CAVIAR AND CHIVES

Elegant minimalism is the spirit of this dish, which uses a bed of delicate angel hair pasta coated in lemon butter as the background for a luxurious dollop of caviar. If you want to go all out, use beluga, sevruga, or ossetra. But domestic golden whitefish caviar, black lumpfish roe, or plump pink salmon roe are also excellent—and more reasonably priced—options.

¾ pound uncooked angel hair pasta
1¼ cups (2½ sticks) unsalted butter,
    cut into pieces
¼ cup fresh lemon juice
½ cup caviar
2 tablespoons finely chopped fresh
    chives

Bring a large pot of salted water to a boil and add the pasta; cook until al dente, following package directions.

Just before the pasta is done, melt the butter in a saucepan over moderate heat. As soon as it has melted, stir in the lemon juice. Arrange the cooked and drained pasta in shallow serving bowls and drizzle the lemon butter over it. Top each serving with a dollop of caviar and a sprinkling of chives.

LEMON-CHAMPAGNE GRANITA

The icy, crystalline sorbet known as a granita gets extra sparkle from a splash of champagne added at serving time. Prepare this dessert a day in advance; take it out of the freezer about 30 minutes before serving to soften to a thick, slushy consistency, or put the solid-frozen mixture in a food processor and pulse the machine until the desired consistency is achieved. Serve in old-fashioned wide champagne glasses or in wine goblets. Top with a few raspberries, if you like.

1 cup water
1 cup superfine sugar
1 cup fresh lemon juice
2 tablespoons grated lemon zest
1–2 cups dry to medium-dry
   champagne or sparkling wine
Fresh mint sprigs, for garnish

In a saucepan, stir together the water and sugar. Bring to a boil over moderate heat, stirring to dissolve the sugar. Boil for 1 minute, pour into a bowl, and let cool to room temperature.

Stir in the lemon juice and zest and pour into a shallow metal pan or pans. Transfer the pan to the freezer. Every 30 minutes to 1 hour, stir the mixture with a fork, scraping ice crystals from the side toward the center, continuing until it forms a thick, scoopable slush.

Scoop the granita into chilled dishes and slowly drizzle champagne over it. Garnish with mint sprigs.

PASTA BY CANDLELIGHT

Serves 4

Asparagus Vinaigrette
Lobster Pasta with Champagne Cream Sauce
Dark Chocolate-Hazelnut Terrine with Raspberry Sauce

This luxurious dinner is perfect for a special celebration for close friends; divide the quantities in half, and you have an ideal romantic dinner for two. Set the table with gleaming silver and china and your best crystal. Pour a dry white wine with the asparagus, and champagne—of course—with the pasta. Brandy or liqueurs, and strong black coffee, may accompany the elegant chocolate dessert.

Most of the preparation may be done several hours before guests arrive: the asparagus cooked, dressed, and chilled; the chocolate terrine melted, molded, and refrigerated. You can even shell and slice the lobster and make the champagne cream sauce shortly before dinner is set to begin, gently rewarming the sauce while the lobster medallions broil.

ASPARAGUS VINAIGRETTE

One of the simplest—and still the best—ways to appreciate the taste and texture of fresh asparagus.

> 1 pound fresh asparagus, tough ends
>   snapped off and discarded
> Lemon Vinaigrette or Balsamic
>   Vinaigrette (pages 7–8)
> 1 tablespoon finely chopped fresh
>   chives or parsley

In a saucepan large enough to hold all the asparagus, bring to a boil enough lightly salted water to cover the asparagus. Add the asparagus and simmer until it is tender-crisp, 3 to 5 minutes. Drain well.

While it is still hot, neatly arrange the asparagus on a serving platter. Drizzle the dressing evenly over the asparagus. Let it cool to room temperature, then cover with plastic wrap and refrigerate until serving time.

Before serving, garnish the asparagus with chopped chives or parsley.

LOBSTER PASTA WITH CHAMPAGNE CREAM SAUCE

You can find fresh or frozen lobster tails in most good seafood markets. Australian rock lobster tails are fine alternatives to domestic lobster. Serve over thin to medium strands or ribbons such as angel hair, spaghetti, linguine, or fettucine.

1¼ pounds lobster tails in the shell
6 tablespoons unsalted butter
3 medium shallots, finely chopped
2 cups dry to medium-dry
    champagne
2 cups heavy cream

¾ pound uncooked pasta
Salt and white pepper
½ tablespoon grated lemon zest
2 tablespoons caviar (optional)
1 tablespoon finely chopped fresh
    chives

Preheat the broiler until very hot.

With the tip of a small, sharp knife, carefully cut lengthwise through the shells along the underside of the lobster tails. With your thumbs, carefully pry apart the shells and peel them away from the meat. Slice the meat crosswise into ½-inch-thick medallions.

In a large skillet or saucepan, melt 4 tablespoons of the butter over moderate heat. Add the shallots and sauté them until tender, 2 to 3 minutes. Add the champagne and bring it to a boil; boil briskly until it reduces by half, 7 to 10 minutes. Stir in the cream and continue boiling until thick and reduced by about a third, about 10 minutes more.

At the same time as the champagne and the cream are reducing, bring a large pot of salted water to a boil and add the pasta; cook until al dente, following package directions.

A few minutes before the sauce is done reducing and the pasta is done cooking, melt the remaining butter in a small saucepan. Brush the lobster medallions with the butter and season lightly with salt and pepper. Broil close to the heat until lightly browned and cooked through, 1 to 2 minutes per side.

Stir the lemon zest into the sauce; taste and adjust the seasonings. On individual plates or bowls, drizzle the sauce over the cooked pasta. Place the lobster medallions on top and garnish with caviar, if you like, and chives.

DARK CHOCOLATE-HAZELNUT TERRINE
WITH RASPBERRY SAUCE

Three intense flavors combine in one luxurious dessert that is made with surprising ease.

> ¼ cup shelled hazelnuts
> ½ cup heavy cream
> ½ pound semisweet chocolate, broken
>   into small pieces
> Raspberry Sauce (page 28)
> Fresh mint sprigs, for garnish

Preheat the oven to 325°F. Spread the hazelnuts on a baking sheet and toast them in the oven for about 10 minutes, until nicely browned. Empty the nuts onto half of a kitchen towel; fold the other half over them and rub them inside the towel to remove their skins. Put the nuts in a food processor or blender and pulse until finely chopped.

Line a miniature, 2-cup loaf pan with waxed paper, cutting or folding the paper to neatly fit the pan's corners.

Put the cream and chocolate in the top of a double boiler or in a saucepan set inside a larger pan of hot water. Stir until the chocolate completely melts and blends with the cream. Sprinkle and stir in the ground hazelnuts.

Pour the chocolate mixture into the lined loaf pan. Cover with plastic wrap and refrigerate for at least 2 hours, until the mixture is solid.

To unmold the terrine, place a flat serving plate on top and invert the pan and plate together; if the terrine won't unmold, dip its bottom briefly in warm water and try again. Peel off the waxed paper.

To serve, spoon the Raspberry Sauce onto individual chilled serving plates. With a sharp knife dipped in warm water, cut the terrine crosswise into ½-inch-thick slices and arrange them on the plates. Garnish with mint sprigs.

MEMORABLE OCCASION CELEBRATION

Serves 4

Steamed Artichokes with Anchovy Mayonnaise
Chargrilled Beef Tenderloin Pasta with Ratatouille Sauce
Mocha Mousse

Serve this menu when there's something special to celebrate—or let its combination of elegant foods make any occasion special. Pour a bone-dry white wine with the artichoke appetizer; then segue to a light- to medium-bodied red with the main pasta course.

Since the artichokes and their dipping sauce are both served chilled, they can be prepared several hours ahead of time; the mousse, too, requires advance preparation. Cook the ratatouille sauce for the pasta in advance, too, if you like, and gently rewarm it while the steak and pasta cook.

STEAMED ARTICHOKES WITH ANCHOVY MAYONNAISE

The rich, sharp-tasting dipping sauce nicely complements the artichokes' subtle-yet-strong flavor.

½ lemon
4 large artichokes
2 2-ounce tins anchovy fillets,
    drained
2 cups good-quality mayonnaise
2 tablespoons fresh lemon juice
3 tablespoons finely chopped fresh
    parsley

Fill a large pot two-thirds full with cold water; squeeze in the juice from the lemon half, and throw in the lemon half. Bring to a boil.

Meanwhile, break off the artichokes' stems, if any remain; with a sharp knife, trim the bottoms flat. Peel off the tough lower petals near the base. With kitchen scissors, trim the sharp tips of the remaining petals.

Put the artichokes in the boiling water and cook until one of the center petals will pull out easily, 30 to 40 minutes. Drain and let cool to room temperature; then refrigerate until chilled.

Put the anchovies in a food processor and pulse until finely chopped. Add the mayonnaise and lemon juice and process until smooth. Pulse in 2 tablespoons of the parsley. Transfer to a bowl, cover with plastic wrap, and refrigerate until serving time.

To serve, place the artichokes on individual serving plates and spoon the dip on the side or in small individual bowls. Garnish the dip with the remaining parsley.

CHARGRILLED BEEF TENDERLOIN PASTA
WITH RATATOUILLE SAUCE

Main course and side dish combine attractively on a single plate, with slices of prime beef draped on top of a colorful Mediterranean-inspired vegetable sauce. Serve over ribbons such as fettucine, mafalde, or tagliatelli.

4 tablespoons olive oil
2 tablespoons fresh lemon juice
1½ pounds beef tenderloin steak, about 1½ inches thick
1 medium onion, finely chopped
1 large shallot, finely chopped
¾ pound Roma tomatoes, stemmed and coarsely chopped
½ pound eggplant, peeled and cut into ½-inch cubes
¼ pound zucchini or golden summer squash, trimmed and cut into ½-inch cubes

1 small green bell pepper, stemmed, seeded, and cut into ½-inch squares
2 tablespoons tomato paste
1 teaspoon sugar
1 teaspoon dried basil
1 teaspoon dried oregano
1 teaspoon dried thyme
1 teaspoon salt
¾ pound uncooked pasta
Salt and freshly ground black pepper
2 tablespoons coarsely chopped fresh Italian parsley

In a shallow bowl, stir together 2 tablespoons of the olive oil with the lemon juice. Turn the steak in the mixture and leave to marinate at room temperature while you prepare the ratatouille sauce. Preheat the broiler.

In a large saucepan, heat the remaining oil over moderate heat. Add the onion and shallot; sauté until tender, about 3 minutes.

Add the vegetables. Sauté just until they begin to exude their juices, 2 to 3 minutes. Stir in the tomato paste, sugar, basil, oregano, thyme, and salt. Simmer until the vegetables are tender-crisp, about 15 minutes.

As soon as the vegetables are simmering, bring a large pot of salted water to a boil and add the pasta; cook until al dente, following package directions.

As soon as the pasta starts cooking, remove the steak from the marinade and season lightly with salt and pepper. Broil 4 to 5 inches from the heat for 5 minutes per side for medium-rare.

Drain the pasta and arrange on individual serving plates. Cut the steak on a diagonal into ¼-inch-thick slices. Spoon the ratatouille over the pasta and drape some steak slices over the sauce. Garnish with parsley.

MOCHA MOUSSE

After a meal of strong flavors, the creaminess of this mousse and its classic combination of chocolate and coffee soothe and satisfy.

1 cup heavy cream
6 ounces semisweet chocolate, broken into coarse pieces
¼ cup hot strong black coffee
½ teaspoon pure vanilla extract

3 egg yolks
6 egg whites, at room temperature
Chocolate-covered espresso beans (optional), for garnish

In a heavy saucepan, heat half the cream over medium heat just until bubbles begin to form around its edges. Set aside.

Put the chocolate in a food processor and pulse until coarsely chopped. With the machine running, pour in the hot coffee and vanilla and continue processing until the chocolate has melted and smoothly blended with the coffee. Scrape down the bowl. With the machine running, pour in the egg yolks and process until smooth. Set aside.

In a mixing bowl, beat the egg whites until they form stiff peaks. With a rubber spatula, gradually fold the chocolate mixture into the egg whites until smoothly blended. Cover the bowl and refrigerate until the mousse is set, about 3 hours.

Before serving, beat the remaining cream until it forms soft peaks. Spoon the mousse into individual serving bowls and garnish with a dollop of whipped cream and, if you like, a few chocolate-covered espresso beans.

SIMPLICITY ITSELF

Serves 4

Sherried Consommé
Grilled Shrimp Pasta with Baby Vegetables
Gingered Melon

The minimal work that goes into this simple menu belies the elegant impression it makes. Sparkling glass tableware will show off the clarity of the consommé and the vibrant colors of the main course and dessert. A full-bodied, oaky chardonnay or a dry blush wine may be poured throughout the meal.

Each dish takes only moments to prepare, with the shrimp and vegetables being briefly marinated and then broiled while the pasta cooks. Toss together the simple melon dessert long enough ahead of time to let the ginger's flavor perfume the fruit.

SHERRIED CONSOMME

A splash of sherry adds instant elegance to good quality chicken broth. To ensure the utmost clarity from canned chicken broth, chill the unopened cans in the refrigerator for at least 30 minutes. When you open them, their fat will have solidified at the top, ready to be removed and discarded. If you want to make the soup a little more substantial, spoon ¼ cup of steamed white rice into each serving cup before pouring in the broth.

> *4 cups clear chicken broth*
> *¼ cup dry or medium-dry sherry*
> *2 tablespoons fresh chives cut into*
> * 1-inch pieces*

In a saucepan over medium heat, bring the broth almost to a boil. Remove the pan from the heat and stir in the sherry. Pour into heated soup cups and float the chives on top.

GRILLED SHRIMP PASTA WITH BABY VEGETABLES

There's something particularly elegant about the colors and forms of the baby vegetables available ever-more-widely in good supermarkets and greengrocers. They form a beautiful still-life background for quickly grilled shrimp. Serve over delicate strands such as angel hair or spaghettini.

1¼ cups olive oil
½ cup fresh lemon juice
2 tablespoons finely shredded fresh basil leaves
1 teaspoon finely chopped fresh oregano leaves
1 teaspoon finely chopped fresh thyme leaves
1¼ pounds medium to large fresh shrimp, peeled and deveined, tail fins left attached
6 ounces baby acorn squash, cut in half horizontally
6 ounces baby zucchini, cut in half lengthwise

6 ounces small Japanese eggplant, trimmed and cut lengthwise into ¼-inch-thick slices
1 small red bell pepper, halved, stemmed, seeded, and cut into 1-inch-wide wedges
¾ pound uncooked pasta
Salt and freshly ground black pepper
½ cup grated Parmesan
1 tablespoon finely chopped fresh chives
1 tablespoon finely chopped fresh Italian parsley

In a measuring cup, stir together ½ cup of the olive oil, the lemon juice, 1 tablespoon of the basil, the oregano, and thyme. Divide the mixture equally between 2 shallow bowls. Put the shrimp in one bowl and the sliced vegetables in the other, and toss well to coat; marinate for 15 to 30 minutes.

Preheat the broiler.

Bring a large pot of salted water to a boil and add the pasta; cook until al dente, following package directions.

Meanwhile, lightly season the vegetables with salt and pepper. Arrange them on the broiler tray and broil close to the heat until golden brown, 4 to 5 minutes per side. Before the vegetables cook on the second side, season the shrimp with salt and pepper and add them to the tray; broil until golden, 1 to 2 minutes per side.

Arrange the cooked and drained pasta on individual serving plates and drizzle with the remaining olive oil. Arrange the vegetables over the pasta and sprinkle them with Parmesan; place the shrimp on top. Garnish with the remaining basil, chives, and parsley.

GINGERED MELON

Pieces of crystallized ginger, or candied ginger in syrup, are available in the Asian food sections of well-stocked supermarkets or in Asian markets. If you can't find them, substitute ½ teaspoon ground ginger and 1 teaspoon confectioner's sugar. Pass a plate of simple cookies—ginger snaps or lemon snaps would be appropriate—alongside.

> *1 large well-chilled ripe cantaloupe,*
> *halved, seeded, and scooped with*
> *a melon baller*
> *2 tablespoons crystallized or drained*
> *candied ginger, very finely chopped*
> *½ tablespoon grated lemon zest*
> *Fresh mint sprigs, for garnish*

In a mixing bowl, toss together the cantaloupe, ginger, and lemon zest. Cover and refrigerate about 1 hour.

Spoon into chilled dessert dishes and garnish with mint.

ITALIAN FLAIR

Serves 4

Salad of Bitter Greens and Toasted Walnuts
Pasta with Grilled Chicken, Goat Cheese, Spinach, and Sun-Dried Tomatoes
Tiramisu with Amaretti

There's a contemporary sense of Mediterranean style in this menu, which features ingredients and recipes—bitter salad greens, goat cheese, sun-dried tomatoes, tiramisu—that have come into vogue in recent years and subsequently proven to have real staying power. The table could appropriately be set with plates and cutlery that reflect the rustic Italian spirit behind these dishes, but more contemporary and stylish settings would not be amiss either. Pour a young, slightly gutsy red wine such as a Beaujolais or Chianti.

Advance work makes an easy meal even simpler to prepare. The dessert can be prepared a day ahead of time. Roast the walnuts for the salad then, too, if you like. Start marinating the chicken for the pasta just before you sit down to the salad; the final cooking of pasta, chicken, and their accompaniments is done in just a few minutes after the first-course dishes are cleared.

SALAD OF BITTER GREENS AND TOASTED WALNUTS

Toasting the walnuts substantially enriches their flavor and makes them slightly crunchy—providing excellent contrast to the tender-textured, slightly bitter salad leaves.

½ cup shelled walnut halves or
   pieces
1 small head curly endive, cored and
   torn into bite-sized pieces
1 small head radicchio, cored and
   torn into bite-sized pieces
1 small Belgian endive, cut crosswise
   into ¼-inch-thick slices
¾ cup packed whole arugula leaves
Balsamic Vinaigrette (page 7)
2 tablespoons finely chopped fresh
   chives

Preheat the oven to 325°F. Spread the walnuts on a baking sheet and toast them in the oven for about 10 minutes, until nicely browned. Remove from the oven, transfer to a bowl, and set aside.

Just before serving, put the salad leaves in a mixing bowl and toss with enough vinaigrette to coat them lightly. Transfer the salad to individual chilled serving plates. Scatter the walnuts on top and garnish with chives.

PASTA WITH GRILLED CHICKEN, GOAT CHEESE, SPINACH, AND SUN-DRIED TOMATOES

Quickly sautéed with olive oil and garlic, the cheese, spinach, and dried tomatoes form an intensely flavorful and colorful background for the marinated and grilled chicken. Serve over medium-sized pasta such as fusilli, bow ties, or shells.

6 tablespoons olive oil
2 tablespoons fresh lemon juice
1 teaspoon dried basil
1 teaspoon dried oregano
1 pound boned and skinned chicken
   breasts
¾ pound uncooked pasta
Salt and freshly ground black pepper
2 medium cloves garlic, finely
   chopped

3 cups packed, shredded fresh
   spinach leaves
1 cup packed, drained sun-dried
   tomatoes, cut with scissors into ¼-
   inch-wide strips
½ pound fresh goat cheese, cut into
   medium-sized chunks
2 tablespoons finely chopped fresh
   Italian parsley

In a mixing bowl, stir together 2 tablespoons of the olive oil with the lemon juice, basil, and oregano. Add the chicken breasts, turn them in the mixture to coat them evenly, and leave to marinate for about 30 minutes.

Preheat the grill or broiler.

Bring a large pot of salted water to a boil and add the pasta; cook until al dente, following package directions.

Meanwhile, season the chicken with salt and pepper and grill or broil until golden, about 7 minutes per side.

When the pasta and chicken are almost done, heat the remaining oil in a large skillet over moderate heat. Add the garlic and, as soon as it sizzles, add the spinach and sun-dried tomatoes. As soon as the spinach wilts, add the goat cheese and stir briefly.

Immediately arrange the cooked and drained pasta on serving plates and spoon the spinach and goat cheese mixture on top; generously season with black pepper. Cut the chicken crosswise into ¼-inch-wide strips and drape them over each portion. Garnish with parsley.

TIRAMISU WITH AMARETTI

Amaretti—the crisp little almond macaroons sold commercially in Italian delis—replace the ladyfingers in this popular dessert.

> *½ pound cream cheese*
> *1 cup confectioner's sugar*
> *1 teaspoon pure vanilla extract*
> *¾ cup heavy cream, chilled*
> *4 dozen large (about 2-inch*
>   *diameter) amaretti*
> *1 cup strong black espresso coffee*
> *¼ cup unsweetened cocoa powder*

In a mixing bowl, beat the cream cheese with an electric mixer until smooth and slightly liquefied. Add the sugar and vanilla and beat until smoothly blended.

In a separate bowl, beat the cream until it forms stiff peaks. With a rubber spatula, fold the whipped cream into the cream cheese mixture.

One at a time, dip half the amaretti into the coffee and place them in a single layer in a straight-sided glass serving bowl. Spread half the cream cheese mixture on top. Put half the cocoa powder in a fine-mesh sieve and shake the sieve over the layer of cheese to dust it evenly. Repeat the process with the remaining amaretti, cheese mixture, and cocoa.

Cover the bowl with plastic wrap and chill in the refrigerator at least 1 hour.

ELEGANT YET INFORMAL

Serves 4

Lime-Marinated Shrimp Skewers
Veal and Porcini Pasta with Red Bell Pepper Cream Sauce
Chocolate Fondue with Strawberries

An elegant occasion needn't necessarily be a formal one. The dishes in this menu, while luxuriously tempting, have a casual air that encourages guests to relax and have a good time. Don't hesitate to serve the food on your best everyday plates. Pour a medium-bodied chardonnay or sparkling wine to accompany both the first and main courses.

Both the first and last courses provide some measure of make-ahead convenience. The shrimp marinate for an hour in the refrigerator. You can prepare the fondue before guests arrive and keep it at room temperature, reheating it briefly over the double boiler before serving. The pasta, on the other hand, is a relatively quick last-minute preparation, begun while you heat up the grill for the shrimp; but don't forget to set the mushrooms soaking ahead of time.

LIME-MARINATED SHRIMP SKEWERS

Fresh shrimp always makes an impression served as a first course. The skewers add a touch of informality and allow an attractive presentation.

> 6 tablespoons olive oil
> 3 tablespoons lime juice
> 2 teaspoons finely shredded fresh
>   basil, or 1 teaspoon dried
> 2 teaspoons finely chopped fresh
>   oregano, or 1 teaspoon dried
> 1½ pounds fresh medium shrimp,
>   shelled and deveined, tail fins left
>   attached
> Salt and white pepper

In a mixing bowl, stir together the olive oil, lime juice, basil, and oregano. Add the shrimp and toss well to coat them. Cover with plastic wrap and marinate in the refrigerator for 1 hour.

Preheat the broiler or grill until very hot. Thread the shrimp on small skewers, passing the skewers through the head and tail end of each shrimp. Season with salt and white pepper and cook close to the heat until golden, 1 to 2 minutes per side.

VEAL AND PORCINI PASTA
WITH RED BELL PEPPER CREAM SAUCE

The rose-colored cream sauce gains a sweet edge from roasted bell pepper to beautifully complement the delicacy of the veal and the meaty flavor of the mushrooms. Serve over delicate strands such as angel hair or spaghettini.

1 ounce dried porcini mushrooms
2 tablespoons unsalted butter
1 tablespoon vegetable oil
2 large shallots, finely chopped
1 pound thin veal scallops, cut into
   ½-inch-wide strips
¼ cup dry white wine
2 cups heavy cream

2 medium red bell peppers, roasted,
   peeled, stemmed, and seeded (page
   8), very finely chopped
½ teaspoon salt
½ teaspoon white pepper
¾ pound uncooked pasta
1½ tablespoons finely chopped fresh
   chives

Put the porcini in a bowl and add enough cold water to cover. Leave them to soak about 15 minutes. Drain the mushrooms and coarsely chop them.

Bring a large pot of salted water to a boil.

Meanwhile, melt the butter with the oil in a large skillet over moderate heat. Add the shallots and sauté until tender, 2 to 3 minutes.

Raise the heat and add the veal. Sauté until lightly browned, 3 to 5 minutes. Remove the veal from the skillet. Add the wine and stir and scrape the skillet with a wooden spoon to deglaze the pan deposits.

Stir in the cream, bell peppers, salt, and white pepper. Raise the heat slightly and simmer until thick, about 10 minutes.

At the same time, cook the pasta in the boiling water until al dente, following package directions.

During the last minute or so of the sauce's simmering, return the veal with the porcini to the skillet to warm through.

Arrange the cooked and drained pasta on individual serving plates and spoon the veal and sauce on top. Garnish with chives.

CHOCOLATE FONDUE WITH STRAWBERRIES

Chocolate fondue combines luxurious elegance with the informality of a communal dessert. If good strawberries are not in season, try chunks of banana, sliced kiwi fruit, or orange segments. Dried fruit, biscotti, and chunks of pound cake or angel food cake are also excellent dippables.

> ¼ pound unsweetened chocolate,
>   broken into small pieces
> ¼ pound semisweet chocolate, broken
>   into small pieces
> 1 cup superfine sugar
> 1 cup heavy cream
> 6 tablespoons unsalted butter, cut
>   into ½-inch pieces
> Pinch of salt
> ¼ cup Grand Marnier or other
>   liqueur
> 2 pints ripe strawberries

Put the chocolates, sugar, cream, butter, and salt in the top of a double boiler over barely simmering water. Stir frequently until the chocolate and butter melt and the sugar dissolves completely to form a smooth, thick sauce, 8 to 10 minutes. Stir in the liqueur.

Arrange the strawberries on a platter and transfer the chocolate mixture to a fondue pot for presentation at table. Provide forks for guests to spear berries and dip them into the fondue.

OLD-WORLD EXOTIC

Serves 4

Simple Salad of Baby Greens (page 14)
Turkey Stroganoff
Marinated Oranges with Cinnamon Syrup

There was a time when such Continental preparations as Stroganoff were the height of elegant, exotic dining. Today, they may seem somewhat old hat. But it still can be fun to indulge—especially when the rich main course is tempered with turkey breast and framed by lighter, simpler first and final courses. To increase the fun, set the most lavish table you can, with deep crimson colors and hints of gold or silver. The main course is equally well suited to a very rich chardonnay or a light- to medium-bodied red wine.

You can and should make the dessert up to a day in advance, giving the oranges time to marinate. The salad and main course are easy, last-minute preparations.

TURKEY STROGANOFF

First created and named for the nineteenth-century Russian gourmet Count Paul Stroganoff, this rich preparation brings old-world elegance to the fresh turkey breast cutlets now widely available in supermarkets. Serve over fettucine or other ribbons.

2 tablespoons unsalted butter
1 tablespoon vegetable oil
2 medium shallots, finely chopped
2 medium cloves garlic, finely chopped
½ pound button mushrooms, cut into ¼-inch-thick slices
¾ pound turkey cutlets, cut into ½-inch-wide strips
Salt and freshly ground black pepper

¼ cup dry white wine
¼ cup chicken broth
1 cup heavy cream
2 tablespoons tomato paste
1 teaspoon sugar
½ cup sour cream, lightly whisked until liquefied
¾ pound uncooked pasta
2 tablespoons finely chopped fresh chives

Bring a large pot of salted water to a boil.

In a large skillet or saucepan, melt 1 tablespoon of the butter with the oil over moderate heat. Add the shallots and garlic. As soon as they sizzle, raise the heat and add the mushrooms. Sauté, stirring continuously, until the mushrooms begin to brown, 3 to 4 minutes.

Remove the mushrooms from the skillet and set aside. Season the turkey strips with salt and pepper. Add the remaining butter to the skillet, raise the heat, and sauté the turkey until lightly browned, 3 to 5 minutes. Add the mushrooms, white wine, and broth; stir and scrape with a wooden spoon to deglaze the pan deposits. Stir in the cream, tomato paste, and sugar. Simmer, stirring occasionally, until the sauce is thick, 7 to 10 minutes.

Meanwhile, add the pasta to the boiling water and cook until al dente, following package directions. Stir the sour cream into the sauce and season to taste with salt and pepper.

Arrange the cooked and drained pasta on individual serving plates, spoon the Stroganoff mixture on top and garnish with chives.

MARINATED ORANGES WITH CINNAMON SYRUP

A simple syrup scented with cinnamon enhances these whole, peeled fresh oranges. Accompany them, if you like, with a scoop of rich vanilla ice cream.

> *1½ cups water*
> *¾ cup sugar*
> *1 cinnamon stick*
> *4 large navel oranges*
> *Fresh mint sprigs, for garnish*

In a small saucepan, stir together the water and sugar; add the cinnamon stick. Bring to a boil over moderate heat, stirring to dissolve the sugar.

The moment the mixture reaches a boil, remove it from the heat. Let cool to room temperature.

Using a sharp knife, peel the oranges, slicing off the fruit segments' outer membranes along with the peel. Put the oranges in a bowl just large enough to hold them. Pour the syrup over the oranges to submerge them; tuck the cinnamon stick into the center of the bowl.

Cover with plastic wrap and refrigerate for at least 2 to 3 hours, or up to 24 hours. Serve each orange whole in a shallow bowl with a shallow pool of syrup. Garnish with mint.

CONTEMPORARY ELAN

Serves 4

Grilled Radicchio
Bay Scallop Pasta with Shallot-Chive Cream Sauce
Lemon-Champagne Granita (page 54)

The revolution in contemporary eating habits has us blissfully eating foods we barely—if at all—knew about a decade or two ago. Witness the popularity of purple-red radicchio, a vegetable long popular in Italy, and the widespread availability of scallops and other seafood once enjoyed only by those who lived near coastal waters. This simple menu celebrates such newfound favorites. Serve it on fine, plain china. Accompany with a bone-dry white wine.

The dessert requires advance preparation the day before to develop its signature icy texture. Start marinating the radicchio up to an hour before serving time, and start the shallot cream sauce when the radicchio begins to cook.

GRILLED RADICCHIO

The marinating and grilling add a sweet, savory edge of flavor to this pleasantly bitter leaf vegetable.

> 6 tablespoons olive oil
> 3 tablespoons balsamic vinegar
> 4 small or 2 medium-to-large heads
>   radicchio, halved lengthwise
> Salt and freshly ground black pepper
> 2 tablespoons finely chopped fresh
>   Italian parsley
> 1 large lemon, cut into quarters

In a shallow dish, stir together the olive oil and vinegar. Turn the radicchio halves in the mixture and leave them cut sides down to marinate at room temperature for 30 minutes to 1 hour.

Preheat the grill or broiler until very hot.

Season the radicchio all over with salt and pepper and grill or broil close to the heat until lightly charred, 2 to 3 minutes per side. Serve on individual plates, garnished with parsley and accompanied by lemon wedges.

BAY SCALLOP PASTA
WITH SHALLOT-CHIVE CREAM SAUCE

Little bay scallops hardly bigger than a thumbnail are widely available in seafood shops and supermarkets. The simple cream sauce highlights their fresh, sweet flavor. Serve over delicate angel hair pasta or other fine strands.

¼ cup (½ stick) unsalted butter, cut
   into pieces
6 medium shallots, finely chopped
4 cups heavy cream
¾ pound uncooked pasta
¾ pound bay scallops, trimmed of
   membranes
3 tablespoons finely chopped fresh
   chives
½ teaspoon salt
¼ teaspoon white pepper
Whole chives, for garnish

In a large saucepan or skillet, melt the butter over moderate heat. Add the shallots and sauté until tender, 2 to 3 minutes.

Add the cream, bring to a boil, and simmer gently until the sauce reduces by about half, 15 to 20 minutes.

About halfway through the simmering, bring a large pot of salted water to a boil and add the pasta; cook until al dente, following package directions.

Stir in the scallops, chives, salt, and pepper and simmer until the scallops are done, 2 to 3 minutes more.

Arrange the cooked and drained pasta on heated serving plates. Spoon the sauce and scallops on top and garnish with whole chives.

4

LAVISH AND HEARTY

....

TRATTORIA SUPPER

Serves 4

Caesar Salad
Classic Lasagna with Meat Sauce
Baked Garlic-Parmesan Toasts
Simple Spumoni (page 36)

Hearts of families and friends alike will warm to a menu so evocative of Italian trattorias that you can almost hear mandolin music playing gently in the background. Set the table with red-checked linens, of course, and rustic plates; while you're at it, meet the clichés head-on and use a wine bottle as a candle-stick. Pour a rough and ready Chianti or other Italian red.

The lasagna may be assembled several hours or a day before, if necessary, to be held in the refrigerator until baking time. Dessert, too, is a make-ahead item. Whip up the butter for the toasts at the last minute, letting them bake in the oven with the lasagna. Dress and toss the crisped lettuce for the salad just before serving. Feel free to put salad, lasagna, and toasts on the table at the same time.

CAESAR SALAD

Though invented by a chef in the Mexican border town of Tijuana, this salad—headily flavored with garlic, anchovies, and Parmesan—has understandably become a popular standby of Italian restaurants. In this particular menu it is served without croutons, which would be redundant with the accompanying toasts. If you'd like to add croutons, simply sauté bread cubes in olive oil with a crushed garlic clove until golden brown; then drain on paper towels. If you have any health concerns about eating lightly cooked egg, leave it out of the recipe.

1 egg, in the shell
2 cloves garlic, finely chopped
4 anchovy fillets
3 tablespoons fresh lemon juice
2 teaspoons Worcestershire sauce
½ cup olive oil
1 medium-sized head romaine
* lettuce, leaves separated, wrapped*
* in a damp towel, and refrigerated*
½ cup grated Parmesan
Freshly ground black pepper

Bring a small saucepan of water to a boil. Add the egg and boil for 1 to 2 minutes. Drain immediately.

In a mixing bowl, use a fork to mash the garlic along with the anchovies until they form a smooth paste. Stir in the lemon juice and Worcestershire. Beating continuously, slowly pour in the olive oil.

With your hands, tear the chilled romaine leaves into bite-sized pieces, putting them in a large salad bowl. Add the dressing, break in the egg, sprinkle on the Parmesan, and add pepper to taste. Toss well to coat the lettuce evenly.

CLASSIC LASAGNA WITH MEAT SAUCE

The layered and baked dish of noodles, thick meat sauce, and creamy cheese may easily win the prize as the most satisfying pasta dish of all.

⅓ pound uncooked lasagna noodles
2 tablespoons olive oil
1 small onion, finely chopped
1 clove garlic, finely chopped
½ pound ground beef
¼ pound sweet or hot Italian
  sausage, casing peeled off and
  discarded
1 16-ounce can crushed tomatoes
2 tablespoons tomato paste

2 teaspoons sugar
1 teaspoon dried basil
1 teaspoon dried oregano
1 teaspoon salt
1 bay leaf
1 cup ricotta cheese
6 tablespoons grated Parmesan
1 egg, lightly beaten
½ pound mozzarella, coarsely
  shredded

Bring a large pot of salted water to a boil and add the lasagna noodles; cook until al dente, following package directions.

In a large skillet or saucepan, heat the oil over moderate heat. Add the onion and garlic and sauté 2 to 3 minutes. Add the beef and sausage and sauté, stirring with a wooden spoon to break up the meat coarsely, until evenly browned, 5 to 7 minutes. Pour off excess fat.

Add the tomatoes, tomato paste, sugar, basil, oregano, salt, and bay leaf. Simmer briskly until thick, 10 to 15 minutes.

Meanwhile, in a mixing bowl, stir together the ricotta, Parmesan, and egg until smooth.

Preheat the oven to 375°F.

Lightly spray a deep 8-inch-square baking dish with nonstick spray. Spread a thin layer of the sauce on the bottom of the dish. Top with one third of the cooked and drained lasagna noodles, trimming to fit. Spread one third of the remaining sauce on top, then a third of the ricotta mixture and a third of the mozzarella. Repeat until all the ingredients are used and the dish is full, ending with the mozzarella.

Cover the dish loosely with foil and bake for about 30 minutes. Remove the foil and bake 20 to 30 minutes more, until the top is golden-brown and bubbly. Remove from the oven and let the lasagna settle for 5 to 10 minutes before slicing and serving.

BAKED GARLIC-PARMESAN TOASTS

An appealingly crisp, crunchy alternative to conventional garlic bread.

¾ cup (1½ sticks) unsalted butter,
   softened
2 cloves garlic, crushed with a garlic
   press
¾ cup grated Parmesan
2 tablespoons finely chopped fresh
   chives
1 narrow (8- to 12-inch) loaf
   Italian-style bread, cut diagonally
   into ½-inch-thick slices

Preheat the oven to 375°F.

In a mixing bowl, use a fork to stir together the butter and garlic. Add the Parmesan and chives and mash until smoothly blended.

Spread the butter-cheese mixture generously on one side of each bread slice. Arrange the slices butter-side up on a baking sheet and bake until golden brown, about 12 minutes. Transfer to a plate or a napkin-lined basket and serve hot.

COLUMBUS DAY PARTY

Serves 4

Salad of White Beans, Tuna, Anchovies, Arugula, and Endive
Italian Sausage and Peppers with Seashell Pasta
Marinated Oranges with Cinnamon Syrup (page 77)

Every day can seem like Columbus Day with this array of flavorful Italian favorites. Serve on simple tableware to show off the bright colors, and pour a robust Italian red wine to complement the pleasantly assertive tastes.

Most of the preparation is done in advance: marinating the white beans; marinating the oranges for dessert; and roasting the bell peppers for the pasta. All the work that remains is the simple assembly of the salads and the quick sautéing of the sauce while the pasta cooks.

SALAD OF WHITE BEANS, TUNA, ANCHOVIES, ARUGULA, AND ENDIVE

Refreshingly bitter arugula and endive leaves transform the traditional Italian tuna-and-white-bean appetizer into a satisfying appetizer salad.

1 14½-ounce can cannellini (white
    kidney) beans, rinsed and drained
Lemon Vinaigrette (page 8)
1 medium clove garlic, crushed with
    a garlic press
2 tablespoons finely chopped fresh
    parsley
3 cups packed arugula leaves
2 medium heads Belgian endive,
    thinly sliced
1 6½-ounce can tuna in oil, drained
1 2-ounce can anchovy fillets,
    drained and separated
2 tablespoons finely chopped fresh
    chives
Freshly ground black pepper

In a mixing bowl, stir together the beans, vinaigrette, garlic, and parsley. Cover with plastic wrap and marinate in the refrigerator for at least 1 hour.

Before serving, arrange a bed of arugula on each serving plate. Scatter the sliced endive in the center. Mound the beans on top of the endive. Break the tuna on top in coarse chunks. Garnish with anchovies, chives, and lots of black pepper.

ITALIAN SAUSAGE AND PEPPERS
WITH SEASHELL PASTA

Use your choice of sweet or hot Italian sausage. Serve over medium-sized shells or other shapes.

¾ *pound uncooked pasta*
¾ *cup olive oil*
1½ *pounds fresh Italian sausage, cut crosswise into ½-inch-thick slices*
4 *medium cloves garlic, finely chopped*
8 *medium bell peppers in assorted colors, roasted, peeled, stemmed, and seeded (page 8), cut or torn into ½-inch-wide strips, juices reserved*
¼ *cup packed finely chopped fresh parsley*

Bring a large pot of salted water to a boil and add the pasta; cook until al dente, following package directions.

Meanwhile, in a large skillet, heat 2 tablespoons of the oil over moderate heat. Add the sausage slices and sauté until evenly browned, 4 to 5 minutes. Remove and set aside; pour off the fat from the skillet.

Add the remaining oil to the skillet over moderate heat. Add the garlic and, as soon as it sizzles, add the peppers and their juices. Sauté about 2 minutes, then stir in the sausage slices and parsley.

Arrange the cooked and drained pasta in a large serving bowl or on individual plates and spoon the peppers and sausage on top.

SUNDAY NIGHT SUPPER

Serves 4

Potted Baby Shrimp with Lemon Parsley Butter
Pumpkin Gnocchi with Gorgonzola Sauce
Cold Baked Apples with Marsala

Give the weekend a grand, family-style finale with a richly satisfying array of easily prepared recipes. This is a time to press the everyday household dishes into service yet again: they'll look like they've gotten a new lease on life thanks to the surprisingly elegant yet satisfying food. A medium-dry white wine would be appropriate to drink, and beer, too, could be poured.

Simple though the work is, most of it can be done hours ahead of time: the shrimp covered with their butter and chilled, the apples baked and refrigerated. Even the gnocchi batter can be made in advance, covered with plastic wrap, and refrigerated for a few hours. Their sauce takes only as long to make as it takes cream to heat and cheese to melt.

POTTED BABY SHRIMP
WITH LEMON PARSLEY BUTTER

Considering how easy it is to make, this refreshing cold appetizer makes quite an elegant impression. Buy little bay shrimp already cooked from your fishmonger. In a pinch, use canned shrimp. Serve with crusty bread or rolls for guests to spread the buttery shrimp mixture on.

½ pound cooked bay shrimp
½ cup (1 stick) unsalted butter, cut
   into pieces
3 tablespoons fresh lemon juice
2 tablespoons finely chopped fresh
   parsley
¼ teaspoon salt
⅛ teaspoon white pepper

Loosely pack the bay shrimp into little 4-ounce ramekins or bowls.

In a small saucepan over low heat, melt the butter. The moment it is melted, remove from the heat and stir in the lemon juice, parsley, salt, and white pepper. Pour the mixture over the shrimp in each ramekin, filling it almost to the rim. Refrigerate until the butter solidifies, at least 1 hour.

About 15 minutes before serving, remove the ramekins from the refrigerator to let the butter soften slightly.

PUMPKIN GNOCCHI WITH GORGONZOLA SAUCE

If you don't want to spend the time making the pumpkin gnocchi, buy ready-to-cook prepared gnocchi from an Italian delicatessen or well-stocked supermarket.

> 1 cup canned pumpkin puree
> 1 large egg, lightly beaten
> 3 cups flour
> 1 teaspoon salt
> ¼ teaspoon ground allspice
> 2 cups heavy cream
> 1¼ pounds Gorgonzola, crumbled
> 1 tablespoon finely chopped fresh
>   chives

In a mixing bowl, stir together the pumpkin and egg. In a separate bowl, combine the flour, salt, and allspice. Stirring continuously, gradually add the dry ingredients to the pumpkin mixture until it forms a thick, moldable paste.

Bring a saucepan of salted water to a boil; reduce the heat to a brisk simmer. With a teaspoon, scoop up balls of the paste and drop them into the water; simmer until they rise to the surface, about 10 minutes.

While the gnocchi are simmering, bring the cream to a boil in a saucepan over moderate heat. Reduce the heat to a simmer and stir in the Gorgonzola. Stir continuously until the cheese melts and the sauce thickens.

Drain the gnocchi and arrange on individual serving plates or in a large bowl. Spoon the cheese sauce over them and garnish with chives.

COLD BAKED APPLES WITH MARSALA

Sweet Italian marsala adds an alluring flavor and color to these refreshing apples.

> 4 large cooking apples, cored, skins
>   scored with a knife
> ½ cup seedless golden or brown
>   raisins
> 1 tablespoon grated orange zest
> 1 tablespoon grated lemon zest
> ¾ cup water
> ½ cup sugar
> ½ cup marsala
> ¾ cup light or heavy cream

Preheat the oven to 350°F.

Put the apples in a baking dish just large enough to hold them. In a small bowl, toss together the raisins and both zests. Spoon the mixture into the center of each apple.

In a small saucepan, stir together the water and sugar. Bring to a boil over moderate heat, reduce the heat slightly, and simmer about 2 minutes more. Remove from the heat and stir in the marsala.

Drizzle the syrup over and around the apples and into their centers. Bake until the apples are tender, about 1 hour, basting 3 or 4 times. Let them cool to room temperature. Then cover and refrigerate until serving time.

Serve in shallow bowls with their syrup; pass cream alongside for guests to drizzle over their servings to taste.

RICH REPAST

Serves 4

Salad of Bitter Greens and Toasted Walnuts (page 68)
Lasagna with Ground Lamb
Mint–Vanilla Bean–Chocolate Chunk Ice Cream

This is a menu of rich surprises, introduced by a palate-cleansing salad studded with walnuts. Though it looks conventional, the lasagna intrigues with a hint of exotic flavors, and a home-churned, refreshing dessert ends the meal. The meal's Middle Eastern overtones call for exotic-looking tableware or accessories. Pour beer or a gutsy red wine.

You can make the ice cream up to a week in advance and assemble the lasagna several hours to a day ahead of time. This leaves only the simple salad assembly and final baking of the main course to put a richly satisfying repast on the table.

LASAGNA WITH GROUND LAMB

Lamb makes an unusual change of pace for lasagna. With the spices added to the ricotta layer, the dish is subtly reminiscent of Greek cuisine.

⅓ pound uncooked lasagna noodles
2 tablespoons vegetable oil
1 small onion, finely chopped
1 clove garlic, finely chopped
½ teaspoon whole dried fennel seeds
1 pound ground lamb
1 16-ounce can crushed tomatoes
2 tablespoons tomato paste
2 teaspoons sugar
1 teaspoon dried oregano

1 teaspoon salt
1 bay leaf
1 cup ricotta cheese
6 tablespoons grated pecorino cheese
½ teaspoon ground cinnamon
⅛ teaspoon grated nutmeg
1 egg, lightly beaten
½ pound mozzarella, coarsely
   shredded

Bring a large pot of salted water to a boil and add the lasagna noodles; cook until al dente, following package directions.

In a large skillet or saucepan, heat the oil over moderate heat. Add the onion, garlic, and fennel seeds and sauté 2 to 3 minutes. Add the lamb and sauté, stirring with a wooden spoon to break up the meat coarsely, until evenly browned, 5 to 7 minutes. Pour off excess fat.

Add the tomatoes, tomato paste, sugar, oregano, salt, and bay leaf. Simmer briskly until thick, 10 to 15 minutes.

Meanwhile, in a mixing bowl, stir together the ricotta, pecorino, cinnamon, nutmeg, and egg until smooth.

Preheat the oven to 375°F.

Lightly spray a deep 8-inch-square baking dish with nonstick spray. Spread a thin layer of the sauce on the bottom of the dish. Top with one third of the cooked lasagna noodles, trimming to fit. Spread one third of the remaining sauce on top, then a third of the ricotta mixture and a third of the mozzarella. Repeat until all the ingredients are used and the dish is full, ending with the mozzarella.

Cover the dish loosely with foil and bake for about 30 minutes. Remove the foil and bake 20 to 30 minutes more, until the top is golden-brown and bubbly. Remove from the oven and let the lasagna settle for 5 to 10 minutes before slicing and serving.

MINT-VANILLA BEAN-CHOCOLATE CHUNK ICE CREAM

Buy a good-quality imported chocolate for this rich, mint-scented ice cream. The recipe yields about ½ gallon—plenty for seconds and thirds.

1 quart heavy cream
¼ cup coarsely chopped fresh mint
1 vanilla bean, split in half
  lengthwise

4 egg yolks
1 cup sugar
½ pound semisweet chocolate,
  coarsely chopped

In a heavy saucepan, warm the cream over moderate heat just until bubbles begin to appear around the edge. Stir in the mint and add the vanilla bean. Cover the pan, remove from the heat, and leave to steep in the cream for about 30 minutes.

In a mixing bowl, beat the egg yolks and sugar until thick and pale yellow, 3 to 5 minutes.

Pour the cream through a strainer set inside a bowl. Discard the mint leaves and vanilla bean. Whisking continuously, slowly pour the cream into the yolk mixture.

Return the mixture to the pan and, over low heat, stir continuously until it is thick enough to coat a wooden spoon, 3 to 5 minutes. Remove the pan from the heat and set its bottom inside a baking pan filled with ice and water. Continue stirring until the mixture cools.

Freeze in an ice-cream maker, following the manufacturer's instructions. When the ice cream is thick but still soft enough to stir, add the chopped chocolate. Serve soft, or transfer to a freezer container and freeze.

BAYOU DINNER

Serves 4

Apple, Ham, Swiss Cheese, and Endive Salad
Cajun-Style Blackened Shrimp and Okra Pasta
Bourbon Bread Pudding

Old and new tastes of Louisiana combine in this robust menu, which begins with a flavorful but palate-soothing salad, continues to a spicy seafood pasta, and ends with a richly indulgent old-fashioned pudding. Present it on your best-loved old dishes or serve with the gleaming silver and china that a grand New Orleans restaurant might use. Offer a spicy medium-dry white wine or a light-bodied young red, or pour a light, well-chilled beer.

You can make the appetizer salad several hours ahead of time and leave it chilling in the refrigerator. Prepare the cream-and-egg mixture for the bread pudding an hour or so in advance, too, keeping it in the refrigerator; pour it over the bread and raisins as guests arrive, so it is ready to put into the preheated oven when you start preparing the pasta main course.

APPLE, HAM, SWISS CHEESE, AND ENDIVE SALAD

Buy a good-quality, country-style sugar-cured ham with a sweet, smoky edge of flavor; your deli's counter assistant should let you take a little taste to make sure you like it.

½ cup mayonnaise
1 tablespoon honey
1 tablespoon cider vinegar
2 tart, crisp green apples, cored,
    quartered, and cut crosswise into
    ¼-inch-wide pieces
2 heads Belgian endive, cut crosswise
    into ¼-inch-wide slices
6 ounces thinly sliced baked ham,
    cut into ¼-inch-wide strips
¼ pound thinly sliced Swiss cheese,
    cut into ¼-inch-wide strips
12–16 whole butter lettuce leaves
2 tablespoons shelled walnut pieces
1 tablespoon finely chopped fresh
    chives or parsley

In a small bowl, stir together the mayonnaise, honey, and vinegar.

In a larger bowl, combine the apple, endive, ham, and cheese. Toss with enough of the mayonnaise dressing to coat generously and bind the salad together. Cover with plastic wrap and refrigerate until serving time.

Arrange the butter lettuce leaves on individual serving plates. Mound the salad in the center of each plate. Garnish with walnuts and chives or parsley.

CAJUN-STYLE BLACKENED SHRIMP AND OKRA PASTA

A nouvelle-inspired version of classic New Orleans cooking. Serve over medium strands or ribbons such as linguine.

¾ teaspoon ground red pepper
½ teaspoon ground white pepper
¼ teaspoon ground cumin
¼ teaspoon salt
1 pound medium-sized shrimp, shelled and deveined
3 tablespoons olive oil
4 medium cloves garlic, finely chopped
1 medium onion, coarsely chopped
½ cup dry white wine
¼ pound fresh okra, trimmed and cut into ½-inch pieces

6 Roma tomatoes, cored and coarsely chopped
1 green bell pepper, halved, stemmed, seeded, and cut into ½-inch chunks
2 teaspoons dried basil
2 teaspoons dried oregano
1 teaspoon sugar
¾ pound uncooked pasta
2 tablespoons finely chopped fresh chives

Bring a large pot of salted water to a boil.

Meanwhile, in a mixing bowl toss together the red and white peppers, cumin, and salt. Add the shrimp and toss to coat them with the spice mixture.

In a large skillet, heat the olive oil over moderate to high heat. When the oil is very hot, add the shrimp and sauté until the spice mixture begins to blacken, 2 to 3 minutes. Add the garlic and onion and sauté about 1 minute more. Add the wine and stir and scrape to deglaze the pan deposits.

Add the okra, tomatoes, bell pepper, basil, oregano, and sugar. Reduce the heat and sauté, stirring frequently, until the okra is tender-crisp, 7 to 10 minutes.

As soon as the okra starts cooking, put the pasta in the boiling water and cook until al dente, following package directions. Drain and arrange on individual plates or in a large serving bowl. Spoon the sauce on top and garnish with chives.

BOURBON BREAD PUDDING

For a really decadent dessert, serve with a scoop of French vanilla ice cream.

1¾ cups light cream
½ cup brown sugar
¼ cup bourbon
¼ cup (½ stick) unsalted butter
2 eggs, lightly beaten
½ teaspoon ground cinnamon
¼ teaspoon grated nutmeg
8 slices slightly stale white bread, cut
    into 1-inch cubes (about 4 cups)
½ cup seedless raisins

Preheat the oven to 350°F.

In a saucepan over low to moderate heat, stir together the cream and sugar. Remove from the heat and stir in the bourbon and butter. In a mixing bowl, beat the eggs with a wire whisk until lightly frothy. Beat in the cinnamon and nutmeg. Whisking continuously, slowly pour in the cream mixture.

Generously grease a 1½-quart baking dish. Toss together the bread and raisins and put them in the dish. Pour the cream-and-egg mixture over the bread. Let stand 10 to 15 minutes.

Bake the pudding in the oven until evenly browned and well set, about 45 minutes. Serve hot or warm, scooped from the baking dish.

BISTRO FEAST

Serves 4

Marinated Peppers and Anchovies
Turkey Scallopini Sauté with Capers and Lemon Cream
Tiramisu with Amaretti (page 70)

Just by their names and the images they conjure in the mind, some dishes seem like the sort you'd order out at a favorite neighborhood restaurant but never go to the trouble of preparing at home. This menu, however, shows how easy such bistro fare can be to cook in your own kitchen. Don't hesitate to serve it on your everyday plates. Pour your own "house wine"—whatever label you consider a reliable standby.

The tiramisu can and the peppers should be prepared up to a day ahead of time. For a lavishly rich pasta sauce, the turkey in lemon cream is a surprisingly easy last-minute creation.

MARINATED PEPPERS AND ANCHOVIES

For the most attractive presentation, use two or more different colors of bell pepper—green, red, yellow, or orange. Serve with crusty bread.

> *2 tablespoons balsamic vinegar*
> *¼ teaspoon salt*
> *1 clove garlic, finely chopped*
> *¼ cup olive oil*
> *4 large bell peppers, roasted, peeled,*
> *   stemmed, and seeded (page 8),*
> *   torn into 1- to 2-inch-wide strips*
> *1 2-ounce tin anchovy fillets,*
> *   drained and separated*
> *2 tablespoons finely chopped parsley*

In a mixing bowl, stir together the vinegar, salt, and garlic until the salt dissolves. Stir in the oil. Add the pepper strips and toss well. Cover with plastic wrap and leave in the refrigerator to marinate for up to 24 hours.

Before serving, arrange the pepper strips on a platter or individual serving plates. Arrange the anchovy fillets on top and garnish with parsley.

TURKEY SCALLOPINI SAUTE WITH CAPERS AND LEMON CREAM

Use the thinly sliced, ready-to-cook boneless and skinless turkey breast—sometimes labeled turkey cutlets—now available in supermarket meat departments. Serve over medium ribbons such as fettucine, fettuccelli, tagliarini, or tagliatelli.

> ¼ cup unsalted butter
> 2 medium shallots, finely chopped
> 1 medium clove garlic, finely chopped
> 1 pound uncooked turkey breast slices, cut into ½-inch-wide strips
> 6 tablespoons fresh lemon juice
> 2 cups heavy cream
> ¾ pound uncooked pasta
> ¼ cup drained capers
> 1 tablespoon grated lemon zest
> 2 tablespoons finely chopped fresh chives
> 2 tablespoons finely chopped fresh parsley

Bring a large pot of salted water to a boil.

In a large skillet, melt the butter over moderate heat. Add the shallots and garlic. As soon as they sizzle, raise the heat, add the turkey, and sauté until lightly browned, 3 to 5 minutes.

Add the lemon juice and stir and scrape with a wooden spoon to deglaze the pan deposits. Add the cream and simmer until thick, 10 to 12 minutes.

As soon as the cream starts simmering, put the pasta in the boiling water and cook until al dente, following package directions.

When the sauce is ready, stir in the capers and lemon zest. Spoon over the cooked and drained pasta and garnish with chives and parsley.

MEXICAN FIESTA

Serves 4

Guacamole and Chips
Mexican-Style Chicken Pasta
Coffee-Orange Flan

The spice and color of Mexico enliven this festive pasta menu. Serve it on your liveliest, most colorful tableware, with brightly hued linens and the most exuberant flowers you can find. Offer a light, slightly chilled red wine or ice-cold Mexican beer.

The flans should be prepared several hours in advance so they can chill, and may be made up to a day ahead of time. Make the guacamole at the last moment for the freshest flavor and brightest color. It takes just a few minutes to mix up and can be prepared after you start the sauce simmering for the main course.

GUACAMOLE AND CHIPS

The popular Mexican avocado dip makes a delightfully casual way to start a meal. If you like, offer crisp raw vegetables for dipping along with the chips.

> *2 large ripe Haas avocados*
> *¼ cup sour cream*
> *2 tablespoons lime juice*
> *Salt and white pepper*
> *2 firm Roma tomatoes, stemmed,*
>   *halved, seeded, and finely chopped*
> *1 small red onion, finely chopped*
> *3 tablespoons canned chopped green*
>   *chili*
> *Tortilla chips or corn chips*

Halve the avocados, remove their pits, and use a tablespoon to scoop out their flesh. In a mixing bowl, use a fork to mash the avocado flesh with the sour cream and lime juice. Season to taste with salt and white pepper.

Fold in the tomatoes, onion, and chili. Transfer to a serving bowl and place on a platter, surrounded by tortilla or corn chips.

MEXICAN-STYLE CHICKEN PASTA

The presence of orange and lime juices, along with chilies, cumin, and cilantro, gives this dish a pleasantly spicy, tropical air. Serve over medium ribbons or your favorite shape such as ruote or rotelli.

3 tablespoons olive oil
2 medium cloves garlic, finely chopped
1 medium red onion, thinly sliced
1 green bell pepper, halved, stemmed, seeded, and cut into ¼-by-1-inch strips
1 long mild green Anaheim chili, halved, stemmed, seeded, and cut crosswise into ¼-inch-wide strips
1 jalapeño chili (optional), halved, stemmed, seeded, and finely chopped
¾ pound boneless, skinless chicken breast, trimmed and cut crosswise into ½-inch-wide strips
½ teaspoon ground cumin
6 tablespoons orange juice
¼ cup lime juice
1 16-ounce can crushed tomatoes
1 tablespoon tomato paste
2 teaspoons sugar
1 teaspoon dried basil
1 teaspoon dried oregano
½ teaspoon salt
¼ teaspoon white pepper
1 bay leaf
¾ pound uncooked pasta
¼ cup finely chopped fresh cilantro

In a large skillet or saucepan, heat half the olive oil over high heat. Add the garlic, onion, bell pepper, and both chilies; sauté until tender and just beginning to brown, about 3 minutes.

Remove the vegetables and set them aside. Add the remaining oil and, still over high heat, sauté the chicken strips until they begin to turn golden, 2 to 3 minutes; sprinkle with the cumin and sauté about 30 seconds more.

Add the orange and lime juices and stir and scrape to deglaze the skillet. Add the tomatoes, tomato paste, sugar, basil, oregano, salt, pepper, and bay leaf. Simmer until thick but still slightly liquid, about 20 minutes.

Meanwhile, bring a large pot of salted water to a boil. Add the pasta and cook until al dente, following package instructions.

Just before serving, stir the cilantro into the sauce. Spoon the sauce over the cooked and drained pasta.

COFFEE-ORANGE FLAN

Flan is one of Mexico's favorite desserts. The distinctive presence of coffee makes it a particularly sophisticated way to end a meal.

1 cup granulated sugar
½ cup water
1 cup heavy cream
1 cup milk
1 tablespoon instant coffee granules
½ tablespoon grated orange zest
½ teaspoon pure vanilla extract
3 eggs
2 egg yolks
½ cup brown sugar
Pinch of salt
Thin strips of orange zest, for
    garnish

Put the granulated sugar and water in a small, heavy saucepan and bring to a boil over moderate heat, stirring constantly until the sugar dissolves. Without stirring, but keeping careful watch, boil the syrup until it caramelizes, turning golden brown, 5 to 7 minutes. Remove from the heat and pour the caramel syrup into 4 individual flan or custard cups, carefully turning each cup to coat its bottom and sides evenly.

In a medium saucepan, heat the cream and milk over moderate heat. As soon as bubbles begin to form on the side, remove the pan from the heat and stir in the coffee, orange zest, and vanilla.

In a mixing bowl, lightly whisk together the eggs, egg yolks, sugar, and salt. Preheat the oven to 325°F. Bring a kettle of water to a boil.

Whisking continuously, slowly pour about a third of the cream mixture into the eggs. Then pour the egg mixture into the saucepan of cream and milk and stir. Pour the resulting mixture into the coated flan cups and put them in a shallow baking pan.

Open the oven, pull out the middle shelf, and place the pan on the shelf. Carefully pour the boiling water into the baking pan until its level comes about halfway up the sides of the flan cups. Slide the shelf into the oven.

Bake the flans until a small, sharp knife inserted into the center of one comes out clean, 20 to 25 minutes. Let them cool to room temperature; then cover and refrigerate.

Serve the flans in their cups, or, for a more stylish presentation, run the tip of a sharp knife around the edge of each cup to loosen the flan. Place a serving plate upside down over each cup; invert cup and plate together, shaking down slightly to dislodge the flan. Carefully lift away the cup. Garnish with orange zest.

SEAFOOD EXTRAVAGANZA

Serves 4

Crab Cakes
Cioppino-Style Seafood Pasta
Assorted Fruit Gellati and Biscotti (page 20)

True seafood lovers can never get enough. That's the rationale behind this menu, which features generous first and main courses of seafood followed by a selection of sorbets to cleanse and refresh the palate. Add a nautical theme to the table, if you like, by using plates or accessories with fish motifs, or form a centerpiece of decorative shells. Pour a crisp white wine with the first course; if you like, you can move on to a brusque young red that will stand up well to the main dish's tomato base.

Prepare and shape the crab-cake mixture up to several hours in advance of the meal, so they're ready to fry when guests arrive. While the crab cakes cook, start sautéing the vegetables for the pasta sauce so it can simmer while guests enjoy the first course.

CRAB CAKES

While good crab cakes need only a squeeze of fresh lemon to embellish them, feel free to serve your favorite cocktail or tartar sauce on the side.

¾ pound cooked crabmeat, flaked and
    picked clean of shell and cartilage
1 egg, beaten
½ cup mayonnaise
¼ cup fine fresh bread crumbs
1 tablespoon finely chopped fresh
    chives
1 tablespoon finely chopped fresh
    parsley
1 teaspoon fresh lemon juice
½ teaspoon sweet paprika
¼ teaspoon salt
¼ teaspoon white pepper
¼ cup all-purpose flour
2 tablespoons unsalted butter
2 tablespoons vegetable oil
1 large lemon, cut into wedges

In a mixing bowl, stir together the crabmeat, egg, mayonnaise, bread crumbs, chives, parsley, lemon juice, paprika, salt, and pepper until they form a thick, moldable paste. Moisten your hands with cold water and shape the mixture into small cakes about 3 inches in diameter and ½- to ¾-inch thick. Place the cakes on a waxed-paper-lined baking sheet, cover loosely with waxed paper, and refrigerate at least 1 hour.

Before serving, lightly dust the crab cakes with the flour. In a large skillet, melt the butter with the oil over moderate heat. Add the crab cakes, taking care not to overcrowd the skillet, and fry until golden brown, 3 to 5 minutes per side. Drain on paper towels and transfer to individual serving plates, accompanied by lemon wedges.

CIOPPINO-STYLE SEAFOOD PASTA

A variation on a traditional seafood stew prepared by San Francisco's Italian fishermen, this dish can be made with whatever fresh fish and shellfish is available and to your liking. Use frozen or canned fish broth, or your own favorite recipe. Serve over medium strands such as linguine or spaghetti.

¼ cup olive oil
3 medium cloves garlic, finely chopped
1 medium onion, finely chopped
1 large green bell pepper, stemmed, seeded, and cut into ½-inch pieces
1–2 teaspoons crushed red pepper flakes
1 teaspoon whole fennel seed
1½ cups fish broth
1 28-ounce can crushed tomatoes
2 tablespoons tomato paste
1 tablespoon sugar

½ tablespoon dried basil
½ tablespoon dried oregano
½ teaspoon salt
1 bay leaf
1 ½-by-2-inch strip orange peel
1 ½-by-2-inch strip lemon peel
¾ pound uncooked pasta
½ pound swordfish fillet, cut into 1-inch pieces
½ pound bay scallops, trimmed
½ pound small shrimp, peeled and deveined

Bring a large pot of salted water to a boil.

Meanwhile, in a large saucepan, heat the oil over moderate heat. Add the garlic, onion, bell pepper, pepper flakes, and fennel seed; sauté about 2 minutes. Add the broth, raise the heat slightly, and simmer briskly until the liquid reduces by about a third, 5 to 7 minutes.

Add the tomatoes, tomato paste, sugar, basil, oregano, salt, bay leaf, and orange and lemon peels. Simmer briskly until the sauce is fairly thick but still somewhat liquid, 12 to 15 minutes more.

While the sauce is simmering, add the pasta to the boiling water and cook until al dente, following package directions.

Stir the swordfish, scallops, and shrimp into the sauce and simmer just until the fish flakes, about 5 minutes. Remove the bay leaf and orange and lemon peels and spoon the sauce over the cooked and drained pasta.

THE MAIN ATTRACTION

Serves 4

Orange and Red Onion Salad (page 46)
Four-Cheese Pasta with Chives and Roasted Walnuts
Lemon Sorbet with Raspberry Sauce (page 28)

A four-cheese sauce may well be the ultimate indulgent topping for pasta—and it is much loved for that very reason. But forming a menu around it can be a challenge. This menu solves the problem by flanking the main attraction with light, slightly acidic tasting first and last courses—one to excite the palate for the dish to come, the other to cleanse and refresh it. Be sure to serve the pasta on a vividly colored dish that contrasts with its monochromatic appearance. Pour a robust white or full-bodied red wine.

The appetizer and dessert are easily prepared well in advance of mealtime. The pasta takes just a few minutes to make from start to finish. Nothing could be easier—or richer.

FOUR-CHEESE PASTA WITH
CHIVES AND ROASTED WALNUTS

The oniony hint of chives and the crunch of the walnuts provide intriguing contrast to the intense creamy richness of the cheese sauce. Substitute your own favorite cheeses in the blend, if you like. Serve over fettucine or other medium ribbons.

½ cup shelled walnut pieces
¾ pound uncooked pasta
2 cups heavy cream
¼ pound Monterey Jack cheese,
   shredded
¼ pound Swiss cheese, shredded
¼ pound blue cheese, crumbled
½ cup grated Parmesan
2 tablespoons finely chopped fresh
   chives

Preheat the oven to 325°F. Spread the walnuts on a baking sheet and toast them in the oven for about 10 minutes, until nicely browned. Remove from the oven, transfer to a bowl, and set aside.

Bring a large pot of salted water to a boil and add the pasta; cook until al dente, following package directions.

Meanwhile, in a medium saucepan, heat the cream over moderate heat. As soon as it is hot but not yet boiling, sprinkle in the cheeses, stirring constantly.

As the cheeses begin to melt, raise the heat slightly and bring the sauce to a boil. Reduce the heat and simmer gently until the sauce is thick and creamy, about 5 minutes. Stir in the chives.

Put the cooked and drained pasta in a large serving bowl and toss it with the sauce. Scatter the toasted walnuts on top.

5

SOMETHING LIGHT

....

WARM-WEATHER SUPPER

Serves 4

Seasonal Melon with Prosciutto (page 18)
Pasta with an Uncooked Sauce of Fresh Tomatoes and Herbs
Cold Mixed Berry Compote with Frozen Yogurt

Some summer days are just too hot to cook. But that doesn't mean you need deprive yourself of a delicious lunchtime or dinner pasta menu—as this trio of dishes tastily proves. The only heat required in the kitchen is for boiling the water to peel the tomatoes and cook the pasta—a task, in fact, that can be accomplished with the same pot of water! Serve on glass dishes or cool white plates, and pour your favorite chilled white, blush, or light red wine.

The only advance work required is tossing the berries and leaving them to mingle their lightly sugared juices for an hour or more in the refrigerator. Assemble the rest of the meal just before serving time, at a cool and leisurely pace.

PASTA WITH AN UNCOOKED SAUCE OF FRESH TOMATOES AND HERBS

Make this sauce when vine-ripened summer tomatoes are at their best. At other times of year, use firm, red, ripe Roma tomatoes. Serve with thin to medium strands, such as angel hair or spaghetti, or with medium shapes such as rotelli or fusilli.

2 tablespoons fresh lemon juice
1 teaspoon salt
½ teaspoon sugar
1 small clove garlic, pressed through
   a garlic press
¼ cup olive oil
1½ pounds firm, vine-ripened
   tomatoes, peeled, cored, halved,
   and seeded (page 9), coarsely
   chopped

2 tablespoons finely shredded fresh
   basil
2 tablespoons finely chopped fresh
   chives
2 tablespoons finely chopped fresh
   Italian parsley
White pepper
¾ pound uncooked pasta

In a mixing bowl, stir together the lemon juice, salt, sugar, and garlic until the salt and sugar dissolve. Stir in the olive oil. Add the tomatoes and herbs and toss well; season to taste with white pepper. Cover and leave at room temperature while you prepare the pasta.

Bring a large pot of salted water to a boil and add the pasta; cook until al dente, following package directions.

Drain the pasta and instantly toss with the tomato mixture. Serve immediately.

COLD MIXED BERRY COMPOTE
WITH FROZEN YOGURT

This uncooked compote makes a perfect warm-weather topping for creamy low-fat frozen yogurt from your best local purveyor. Use whatever fresh berries are at their peak at your supermarket or greengrocer. The light sprinkling of sugar draws out their juices to make the compote's syrup.

> 2 pints mixed ripe berries, small
>   ones left whole, larger strawberries
>   sliced ¼- to ½-inch thick
> 6 tablespoons confectioner's sugar
> 2 tablespoons grated lemon zest
> 2 tablespoons grated orange zest
> 1 quart good-quality vanilla or other
>   flavor frozen yogurt
> Fresh mint sprigs, for garnish

Put the berries in a large mixing bowl and sprinkle evenly with the sugar, lemon zest, and orange zest. Toss gently but thoroughly, then cover with plastic wrap and refrigerate for at least 1 hour.

At serving time, scoop the frozen yogurt into individual chilled dishes and generously spoon the berries and their juices on top. Garnish with mint.

FOR THE GOURMET DIETER

Serves 4

Sherried Consommé (page 64)
Grilled Salmon Pasta with Baby Vegetables
Lemon Zest Meringues

Whoever said that dieters have to suffer? This menu offers gourmet-style sophistication with foods that not only are light but also satisfy the senses. Emphasize their style with your most elegant place settings. And, if you can, allow the indulgence of a glass of white or sparkling wine.

The dessert meringues may be made several hours or a day ahead of time and their platter of fruits prepared an hour or so before the meal. Start marinating the salmon, preparing its vegetables, and heating the broiler and the water for the pasta just before you simmer the consommé and serve it. Then cook the main course after you've cleared away the first-course dishes.

GRILLED SALMON PASTA WITH BABY VEGETABLES

Elegantly simple, delicate pasta strands are tossed with lightly sautéed vegetables and topped with grilled salmon fillets. If you can't find baby vegetables, substitute the smallest, freshest specimens available. Serve on angel hair or other delicate strands.

6 tablespoons olive oil
¼ cup fresh lemon juice
1 pound fresh salmon fillet, cut into 4 equal pieces
¾ pound uncooked pasta
Salt and white pepper
6 ounces baby zucchini, thinly sliced lengthwise
6 ounces baby acorn squash, thinly sliced

6 ounces baby carrots, thinly sliced diagonally
2 ounces button mushrooms, thinly sliced
1½ tablespoons finely shredded fresh basil
1½ tablespoons finely chopped fresh chives
1½ tablespoons finely chopped fresh parsley

In a shallow bowl, stir together 2 tablespoons of the olive oil and half the lemon juice. Turn the salmon fillets in the mixture and leave to marinate at room temperature about 30 minutes.

Preheat the broiler.

Bring a large pot of salted water to a boil and add the pasta; cook until al dente, following package directions.

As soon as the pasta starts cooking, remove the salmon from the marinade and season lightly with salt and white pepper. Broil close to the heat until golden brown, about 3 minutes per side.

As soon as the salmon starts cooking, heat the remaining oil in a large skillet or wok over moderate to high heat. Add the vegetables and sauté until tender-crisp and lightly browned, 3 to 5 minutes. Sprinkle the remaining lemon juice over the vegetables and season to taste with salt and white pepper.

In a mixing bowl, toss the cooked and drained pasta with the vegetable mixture and herbs. Arrange the pasta on individual plates and place the grilled salmon on top.

LEMON ZEST MERINGUES

Serve a plate piled high with these ultra-light yet satisfying cookielike puffs with a platter of the juiciest, most beautiful seasonal fruits you can find.

2 large egg whites
2 teaspoons fresh lemon juice
¼ teaspoon cream of tartar
⅔ cup granulated sugar
1 tablespoon grated lemon zest

Preheat the oven to 275°F.

In a mixing bowl, use an electric beater to beat the egg whites with the lemon juice and cream of tartar until they form soft peaks. Beating continuously, add the sugar little by little and continue beating until it is fully incorporated and the mixture forms stiff peaks; add the lemon zest with the last addition of sugar.

Drop generous tablespoons of the egg-white mixture onto a greased baking sheet. Bake in the oven until the meringues look dry and set, about 30 minutes. With a spatula, transfer the meringues to a wire rack to cool. Store in an airtight container.

HEALTH-CONSCIOUS WINTER MENU

Serves 4

Warm Mushroom Salad
Crab Cannelloni Napolitano
Light Zabaglione

Winter calls for foods that warm and sustain us—hardly the formula, at first glance, for a healthy meal. But the recipes in this menu demonstrate that health-conscious food can be comfort food as well: a rich, savory, warm mushroom salad; a baked dish of pasta tubes stuffed with seafood and ricotta; and a lightened version of a classic Italian egg dessert. Serve the meal on chunky, homestyle crockery. Sip a light to medium-bodied red wine.

Though the first and last courses are quick last-minute creations, the sauce and filling for the pasta course may be prepared in advance and the cannelloni boiled and stuffed; cover the filled baking dish with foil and refrigerate, putting it in the oven to bake about half an hour before mealtime.

WARM MUSHROOM SALAD

Everyday mushrooms gain an elegant edge of texture and flavor by their quick sautéing, and the hot dressing slightly wilts the salad greens.

> 2 cups coarsely torn radicchio leaves
> 2 cups coarsely torn red leaf lettuce
>   leaves
> 2 cups coarsely torn butter lettuce
>   leaves
> 2 tablespoons olive oil
> 2 tablespoons walnut oil
> 1 pound large cultivated mushrooms,
>   cut into ½-inch-thick slices
> 1 shallot, finely chopped
> 2 tablespoons sherry vinegar
> 2 tablespoons finely chopped fresh
>   chives
> 2 tablespoons finely chopped fresh
>   parsley
> ¼ teaspoon salt
> Freshly ground black pepper

Toss the salad leaves together and arrange them in beds on individual serving plates.

In a large skillet, heat the olive and walnut oils over high heat. Add the mushrooms and shallot and sauté until they begin to turn golden, about 3 minutes. Stir in the vinegar, chives, parsley, and salt; season to taste with black pepper.

Spoon the mushrooms and pan juices over the salad leaves and serve immediately.

CRAB CANNELLONI NAPOLITANO

A light yet satisfying crab-and-ricotta mixture fills these pasta tubes, baked in a simple tomato sauce.

NAPOLITANO SAUCE
2 tablespoons olive oil
2 large shallots, finely chopped
1 clove garlic, finely chopped
1 16-ounce can crushed tomatoes
1 tablespoon tomato paste
1 teaspoon dried basil
1 teaspoon dried oregano
1 teaspoon sugar
½ teaspoon salt
1 bay leaf

CRAB CANNELLONI
8 dried cannelloni tubes
2 tablespoons unsalted butter
1 medium onion, finely chopped
1 pound cooked flaked crabmeat, all
   shell and cartilage removed
½ cup ricotta cheese
½ cup soft bread crumbs
¼ cup grated Parmesan
2 tablespoons finely chopped fresh
   parsley
2 eggs, lightly beaten

To make the Napolitano Sauce: in a medium skillet or saucepan, heat the oil over moderate heat. Add the shallots and garlic; sauté until tender, 2 to 3 minutes. Stir in the tomatoes and remaining ingredients. Raise the heat slightly and simmer the sauce until thick, about 15 minutes. Set aside.

To make the Crab Cannelloni: bring a large pot of salted water to a boil and add the cannelloni tubes; cook until al dente, following package directions. Drain and set aside.

Preheat the oven to 350°F.

In a small skillet, melt the butter over moderate heat. Add the onion and sauté until tender, 3 to 5 minutes. In a mixing bowl, stir together the onion, crabmeat, and remaining ingredients.

Spoon the crab mixture into the cooked cannelloni tubes and place them side by side in a greased shallow baking dish just large enough to hold them. Spoon any remaining stuffing around the cannelloni. Spoon the Napolitano Sauce on top, cover with foil, and bake about 30 minutes; uncover the dish and bake about 15 minutes more.

LIGHT ZABAGLIONE

Usually, zabaglione is made with egg yolks alone; here, egg whites lighten the mixture. The quick, frothy, warm sauce, often served on its own with biscotti, is delicious used as a sauce for sliced fresh fruit. Whip it up just before serving. If you like, spoon it over cut-up fresh fruit.

2 eggs, lightly beaten
1 egg yolk
¼ cup sugar
½ cup marsala
2 tablespoons grated lemon zest

Bring a medium saucepan half-filled with water to a boil; reduce the heat to maintain a simmer.

Put the eggs, egg yolk, sugar, marsala, and lemon zest in a heatproof bowl large enough to rest just inside the rim of the pan without touching the water. Place the bowl on top of the pan and, with a wire whisk or electric beater on slow speed, beat the egg-yolk mixture until it is thick and frothy, forming soft peaks when the beater is lifted out.

VEGETARIAN SPECIAL

Serves 4

Vegetable Straciatelle
Mushroom and Fresh Herb Bolognese
Fresh Fruit with Ricotta and Raspberry Sauce

The vegetarian recipes in this menu taste every bit as full-flavored and satisfying as a meat-eater's meal. The trick is the intensity of flavors built up in each recipe: long-simmered vegetable broth, meaty sautéed mushrooms, and light yet rich cheese complemented by a fresh raspberry sauce. Set the table with simple, perhaps white, dishware to show off the colors, or serve on a floral, vegetable, or fruit pattern to emphasize the vegetarian theme. Dry to medium-dry white or blush wine will complement all the flavors.

Each course has make-ahead potential. The vegetable broth can be prepared and refrigerated up to a day before, as can the mushroom Bolognese sauce and the dessert's Raspberry Sauce.

VEGETABLE STRACIATELLE

A vegetarian version of the classic Roman soup whose name, "little rags," describes the wisps of beaten egg that float in the broth. If you're not strictly vegetarian, feel free to use chicken broth.

1 large carrot, thinly sliced
1 large stalk celery, thinly sliced
1 large leek, thinly sliced
1 large onion, thinly sliced
1 whole clove garlic, unpeeled
3 sprigs fresh parsley
1 sprig fresh thyme
1 bay leaf
2 quarts water
¼ teaspoon whole white peppercorns
Salt
3 eggs, beaten
¼ cup Parmesan
2 tablespoons finely chopped fresh
  chives

In a large stockpot, put the vegetables, garlic, parsley, thyme, and bay leaf. Add the water and peppercorns.

Over low to medium heat, slowly bring the liquid to a simmer, regularly skimming it. Continue simmering, partly covered, for 1 to 1½ hours.

Line a sieve or strainer with a double layer of dampened cheesecloth and set it inside a large bowl. Pour the contents of the pot into the strainer. Discard the solids. Lightly season the broth to taste with salt.

Put the broth in a medium saucepan and bring it back to a boil. Reduce the heat to a bare simmer.

In a mixing bowl, stir together the eggs and Parmesan. Drizzle the mixture into the simmering broth, stirring to break it up into thin wisps.

As soon as the egg has cooked, ladle the soup into soup bowls or plates and garnish with chives.

MUSHROOM AND FRESH HERB BOLOGNESE

Common cultivated mushrooms take the role of meat in this satisfying sauce. Serve with medium strands or ribbons such as spaghetti or fettucine.

¼ cup olive oil
2 medium cloves garlic, finely chopped
1 medium onion, finely chopped
2 pounds cultivated mushrooms, coarsely chopped
1 16-ounce can crushed tomatoes
1 tablespoon tomato paste
1 tablespoon finely chopped fresh basil
1 tablespoon finely chopped fresh oregano
1 tablespoon finely chopped fresh thyme
1 tablespoon finely chopped fresh parsley
2 teaspoons sugar
½ teaspoon salt
¾ pound uncooked pasta

In a large skillet, heat the olive oil over moderate to high heat. Add the garlic and onion and, as soon as they sizzle, stir in the mushrooms; sauté, stirring frequently, until all their liquid evaporates and they begin to brown, 10 to 15 minutes.

Stir in the tomatoes, tomato paste, herbs, sugar, and salt. Simmer until the sauce is thick but still slightly liquid, 10 to 15 minutes.

While the sauce is simmering, bring a large pot of salted water to a boil and add the pasta; cook until al dente, following package directions.

Arrange the cooked and drained pasta in a large bowl or on individual plates and spoon the sauce on top.

FRESH FRUIT WITH RICOTTA AND RASPBERRY SAUCE

Though low in fat and fairly light in texture, ricotta cheese has a wonderfully satisfying richness that makes it an ideal foil for fruit in this refreshing dessert.

> *Raspberry Sauce (page 28)*
> *2 cups low-fat ricotta cheese*
> *3 cups mixed fresh soft fruit (berries,*
>   *pitted cherries, kiwi, nectarines,*
>   *peaches, pineapple, plums), cut*
>   *into bite-sized chunks*
> *Fresh mint sprigs, for garnish*

Pour a pool of Raspberry Sauce onto each chilled dessert plate. Place a scoop of ricotta in the center of each plate and arrange the fresh fruit on top of and around the cheese. Garnish with mint sprigs.

REFRESHING TASTES

Serves 4

Tonno e Fagioli
Unbaked Spinach-and-Ricotta Lasagna
Gingered Melon (page 66)

The simply prepared dishes in this menu provide the palate with a refreshing change of pace: a colorful, classic Italian appetizer; a vegetarian lasagna that requires no baking; and a fresh, sweetly spiced dessert. Choose brightly colored or clear glass tableware to present the meal. Sparkling wine or white wine spritzers would be an appropriate choice of beverage.

If you like, prepare the appetizer salad an hour or two before the meal. The tomato sauce for the lasagna may also be prepared ahead and refrigerated, to be gently warmed just before serving time. The melon dessert, though a quick last-minute preparation, benefits from an hour or so in the refrigerator to allow its flavors to mingle.

TONNO E FAGIOLI

Thanks to the good quality of canned Italian cannellini beans, one of Italy's classic antipasti could not be easier to make. If cannellini are unavailable, use any canned white beans. Italian tuna packed in olive oil has the best flavor for this dish, but you could use regular oil-packed or water-packed tuna if you wish.

16 radicchio leaves
2 cups drained canned cannellini
  (white kidney) beans
2 6-ounce cans Italian-style tuna
  packed in olive oil, drained
1 medium red onion, thinly sliced,
  rings separated
2 tablespoons finely chopped fresh
  parsley
1 large lemon, cut into wedges
Freshly ground black pepper

Arrange the radicchio leaves on individual serving plates. Place a bed of beans in the center of each plate and break the tuna into coarse chunks on top. Arrange onion rings over the tuna and garnish with parsley. Place a lemon wedge on each plate for each guest to squeeze over the beans, tuna, and onion; offer black pepper to taste at table.

UNBAKED SPINACH-AND-RICOTTA LASAGNA

Imagine this as a kind of deconstructivist lasagna, assembled on the individual plates.

Napolitano Sauce (page 125)
¾ pound uncooked lasagna noodles
¼ cup (½ stick) unsalted butter
2 tablespoons olive oil
2 large shallots, finely chopped
2 bunches spinach, stemmed, ribbed,
*   and thoroughly washed, leaves cut*
*   crosswise into ¼-inch-wide strips*
Salt and white pepper
1 cup ricotta cheese
6 tablespoons grated Parmesan
2 tablespoons finely chopped fresh
*   parsley*

Prepare the Napolitano Sauce. While it simmers, bring a large pot of salted water to a boil and add the pasta; cook until al dente, following package directions.

While the sauce and pasta are cooking, melt the butter with the oil in a large skillet over moderate to high heat. Add the shallots and, as soon as they sizzle, add the spinach. Sauté, stirring continuously, until the spinach has wilted completely, 2 to 3 minutes; season to taste with salt and white pepper.

Add the ricotta, breaking it up into small clumps with a wooden spoon. Remove from the heat as soon as it begins to melt.

On individual serving plates, layer the lasagna noodles and the spinach-ricotta mixture. Spoon the Napolitano Sauce on top, sprinkle with Parmesan, and garnish with parsley.

NUOVA CUCINA

Serves 4

Stuffed Mushrooms with Ricotta-Parmesan Soufflé
Pasta with Bell Pepper–Marinara Sauce and Grilled Lemon-Herb Chicken
Lemon-Ginger Mousse

There's an updated Italian flair to the simple dishes in this menu: mushrooms baked with a light, soufflé-like cheese stuffing; grilled chicken atop pasta dressed with a colorful bell-pepper sauce; and a sprightly yet rich mousse for dessert. Trot out your trendiest plates for this one, or serve on classic trattoria white china. Pour Chianti or another light red wine.

The mousse requires preparation several hours in advance to allow it to chill and set; you can also make the bell-pepper sauce for the chicken ahead of time and marinate the chicken covered in the refrigerator for up to a few hours. But mix the mushroom stuffing and fill the caps just before baking and serving them.

STUFFED MUSHROOMS
WITH RICOTTA-PARMESAN SOUFFLE

Old-fashioned stuffed mushrooms get light Italian flair from the herbed ricotta-Parmesan-egg mixture.

> *2 eggs, separated*
> *1 cup ricotta cheese*
> *½ cup grated Parmesan*
> *2 tablespoons finely chopped fresh chives*
> *2 tablespoons finely chopped fresh parsley*
> *½ teaspoon white pepper*
> *16–24 large cultivated mushrooms, stems removed*

Preheat the oven to 375°F.

In a mixing bowl, beat the egg whites until they form soft peaks. In a separate bowl, use a fork to mash together the egg yolks, ricotta, Parmesan, chives, parsley, and white pepper until smooth. With a rubber spatula, fold the egg whites into the ricotta mixture.

Spoon the mixture generously into the mushroom caps, placing them in a shallow, lightly greased baking dish. Bake until the ricotta filling is puffed and golden, 20 to 25 minutes. Serve hot.

PASTA WITH BELL PEPPER–MARINARA SAUCE
AND GRILLED LEMON-HERB CHICKEN

The sauce provides a colorful and flavorful background for strips of marinated, quickly grilled or broiled chicken. Serve over medium strands or ribbons such as spaghetti, tagliatelli, or fettucine.

GRILLED LEMON-HERB CHICKEN

3 tablespoons olive oil
3 tablespoons fresh lemon juice
1 teaspoon dried basil
1 teaspoon dried oregano
1 teaspoon dried rosemary
4 boneless, skinless chicken breast halves, about 6 ounces each
Salt and freshly ground black pepper

BELL PEPPER–MARINARA SAUCE

3 tablespoons olive oil
2 medium cloves garlic, finely chopped
1 small onion, finely chopped
1 medium green bell pepper, quartered, stemmed, seeded, and cut crosswise into ¼-inch-wide strips
1 medium red or yellow bell pepper, quartered, stemmed, seeded, and cut crosswise into ¼-inch-wide strips
1 16-ounce can crushed tomatoes
1 tablespoon tomato paste
2 teaspoons sugar
1 teaspoon dried basil
1 teaspoon dried oregano

¾ pound uncooked pasta

For the Grilled Lemon-Herb Chicken: in a mixing bowl, stir together the oil, lemon juice, and herbs. Turn the chicken breasts in the mixture and marinate at room temperature 15 to 30 minutes.

Preheat the grill or broiler, and bring a large pot of salted water to a boil.

Season the chicken with salt and pepper, and grill or broil until golden, about 7 minutes per side.

As soon as the chicken starts broiling, prepare the Bell Pepper–Marinara Sauce. Heat the oil in a large skillet or saucepan over moderate heat. Add the garlic and onion and, as soon as they sizzle, add the bell peppers. Sauté until they just begin to turn tender, 3 to 4 minutes. Add the tomatoes, tomato paste, sugar, basil, and oregano. Simmer until the sauce is thick but still fairly liquid, about 10 minutes more.

While the sauce is simmering, cook the pasta until al dente, following package instructions.

Arrange the cooked and drained pasta on individual serving plates. Season the sauce to taste with salt and pepper and spoon it over the pasta. Cut each chicken breast crosswise into ¼-inch-wide strips and place them on top of the sauce.

LEMON-GINGER MOUSSE

Lemon and ginger are natural companions in sweet desserts, leaving the palate light and refreshed even in a dessert as rich as this mousse.

> 2 teaspoons unflavored powdered
>   gelatin
> ¼ cup warm water
> 6 tablespoons fresh lemon juice
> 1 tablespoon grated lemon zest
> 1 tablespoon grated fresh ginger root
> 3 large eggs
> ¾ cup sugar
> Pinch of salt
> ½ cup whipping cream, chilled
> 2 tablespoons finely chopped
>   crystallized or drained candied
>   ginger (optional), for garnish
> Fresh mint sprigs, for garnish

In a small bowl, stir the gelatin into the water and leave until fully dissolved, about 5 minutes. Stir the lemon juice, lemon zest, and ginger into the gelatin and set aside.

Put the eggs, sugar, and salt in a mixing bowl and beat with an electric beater at high speed until very thick and foamy, about 7 minutes. Reduce the speed to low and slowly pour in the lemon-gelatin mixture, beating until well blended. Cover with plastic wrap and refrigerate until the mixture begins to gel but is still liquid, 45 minutes to 1 hour.

In another bowl, whip the cream until it forms soft peaks. With a rubber spatula, fold it into the chilled lemon mixture. Divide the mixture among individual serving bowls, cover with plastic wrap, and refrigerate until fully set, at least 2 hours.

Before serving, garnish with chopped ginger, if desired, and mint sprigs.

TRATTORIA LIGHT

Serves 4

Trattoria Vegetable Salad
Ground Turkey Pasta Puttanesca
Lemon Sorbet with Raspberry Sauce (page 28)

Thanks to a few clever substitutions, this menu lets you eat lighter without losing the sense of *abbondanza* that accompanies an Italian trattoria-style meal. The antipasto-style salad is so full of color, texture, and flavor that you'd hardly notice it's lacking meat; and ground turkey, a new favorite of health-conscious cooks, brings a robust quality to a traditional peasant-style pasta sauce. Use your everyday dishes, and pour a bargain bottle of Chianti or other red wine.

Both first and last courses are make-ahead dishes, and the turkey sauce may also be cooked ahead of time, which leaves boiling a pot of water and throwing in the pasta as the only strenuous cooking activity to be done before mealtime!

TRATTORIA VEGETABLE SALAD

Reminiscent of an antipasto salad, this quickly tossed together vegetable mixture gains flavor from a couple of hours of marination in the refrigerator.

1 cup drained canned garbanzo
    beans
1 cup drained canned pitted black
    olives, cut into halves
1 cup drained canned artichoke
    hearts, cut into quarters
¼ pound thinly sliced provolone
    cheese, cut into ¼-inch-wide strips
1 large red bell pepper, roasted,
    peeled, stemmed, and seeded (page
    8), torn into ¼-inch-wide strips
2 tablespoons finely chopped fresh
    chives
2 tablespoons finely chopped fresh
    parsley
Lemon Vinaigrette or Balsamic
    Vinaigrette (pages 7–8)
6 cups thinly shredded romaine
    lettuce
Fresh parsley sprigs, for garnish

In a mixing bowl, toss the garbanzos, olives, artichoke hearts, cheese, bell pepper, chives, and parsley with enough vinaigrette to coat them generously. Cover with plastic wrap and refrigerate 1 to 2 hours.

Before serving, arrange the shredded lettuce in beds on individual serving plates and mound the marinated vegetable mixture in the center. Garnish with parsley sprigs.

GROUND TURKEY PASTA PUTTANESCA

The so-called "whore-style" pasta sauce, coarsely thrown together and spiced up by crushed red pepper, gains a wholesome new outlook from ground turkey. Serve over medium strands, ribbons, shells, or other shapes.

2 tablespoons olive oil
3 medium cloves garlic, finely
    chopped
2 medium onions, coarsely chopped
1 green bell pepper, halved,
    stemmed, seeded, and coarsely
    chopped
½ teaspoon crushed red pepper
    flakes
¾ pound ground turkey
1 16-ounce can crushed tomatoes

½ cup dry red wine
2 tablespoons drained whole capers
1 tablespoon tomato paste
2 teaspoons dried basil
2 teaspoons dried oregano
2 teaspoons sugar
1 teaspoon freshly ground black
    pepper
½ teaspoon salt
¾ pound uncooked pasta

In a large skillet, heat the oil over moderate heat. Add the garlic, onions, bell pepper, and pepper flakes. As soon as they sizzle, add the turkey and sauté, stirring and breaking up the meat with a wooden spoon, until it begins to brown, 5 to 7 minutes.

Add the tomatoes, wine, capers, tomato paste, basil, oregano, sugar, black pepper, and salt. Simmer, stirring and scraping to deglaze the pan, until the sauce is thick but still slightly liquid, 20 to 25 minutes.

While the sauce is simmering, bring a large pot of salted water to a boil and cook the pasta until al dente, following package instructions.

Arrange the cooked and drained pasta in a large serving bowl or individual pasta bowls and spoon the sauce on top.

ROBUST FARE

Serves 4

Tricolor Salad with Anchovies (page 22)
Pasta with Lentils and Canadian Bacon
Yogurt-and-Berry Fool

Some of the healthiest dishes imaginable are rustic, traditional ones, such as those in this menu, that make use of quality seasonal produce and know-how to stretch a little rich food a long way. Serve the first two courses on country-style earthenware, the dessert in sparkling glassware. Accompany with red wine or chilled beer.

Make the dessert several hours in advance of the meal, and assemble the salad about 30 minutes before serving. The lentils will be at their best if you start cooking them after you've put the salads together.

PASTA WITH LENTILS AND CANADIAN BACON

Heartwarming and homey, this rustic dish has just a hint of Middle Eastern flavor to it. Canadian bacon, by the way, is surprisingly lean and combines with the lentils and pasta to make a low-fat, high-fiber, healthy main course. Serve with medium-sized pasta shapes such as rotelli, ruote, fusilli, macaroni, or shells.

2 tablespoons olive oil
2 medium cloves garlic, finely chopped
1 medium onion, finely chopped
1 medium carrot, finely chopped
1 medium stalk celery, finely chopped
1 teaspoon ground coriander
1 teaspoon ground cumin
3 cups low-fat chicken broth
¾ cup pink or green lentils, sorted and rinsed

¾ pound Canadian bacon, cut into ¼- to ½-inch dice
1 teaspoon dried marjoram
1 teaspoon dried thyme
¾ teaspoon salt
½ teaspoon freshly ground black pepper
1 bay leaf
¾ pound uncooked pasta
2 tablespoons finely chopped fresh parsley
1 lemon, cut into wedges

In a medium saucepan, heat the oil over moderate heat. Add the garlic, onion, carrot, and celery and sauté until the onion and garlic are translucent, 3 to 5 minutes. Add the coriander and cumin and sauté 1 minute more.

Stir in the broth, lentils, bacon, marjoram, thyme, salt, pepper, and bay leaf. Bring to a boil, then reduce the heat and simmer until the lentils are tender, about 30 minutes.

Meanwhile, bring a large pot of salted water to a boil and add the pasta; cook until al dente, following package directions.

Put the cooked and drained pasta in individual shallow serving bowls and spoon the lentils and Canadian bacon on top. Garnish with parsley and pass lemon wedges for guests to squeeze over individual portions.

YOGURT-AND-BERRY FOOL

Low-fat yogurt replaces the usual cream in this traditional English dessert.

1 pint very ripe strawberries, hulled
½ cup confectioner's sugar
2 tablespoons grated lemon zest
1½ cups low-fat plain yogurt
Fresh mint sprigs, for garnish

In a mixing bowl, use a fork or potato masher to coarsely mash the berries with the sugar and lemon zest.

In a separate bowl, use a wire whisk or an electric beater on low speed to beat the yogurt until slightly liquefied. Add the berries and beat until the yogurt and berries are well blended but small chunks of berry still remain.

Spoon the mixture into tall individual dessert glasses, wine glasses, or dishes. Cover with plastic wrap and chill in the refrigerator for at least 2 hours. Garnish with mint sprigs before serving.

MANDARIN MINCEUR

Serves 4

Velvet Chicken–Sweet Corn Soup
Chinese-Style Ginger-Beef and Vegetable Stir-Fry with Lo Mein
Mandarin Gelatin

Chinese food has long reigned as one of the world's healthiest cuisines—relying on complex carbohydrates like rice and noodles, and stretching small quantities of protein with abundant vegetables. This menu, though seemingly luxurious, is nevertheless admirably light. Serve it on plates with Asian-inspired motifs, and pour your favorite light beer to go with it.

Like most Chinese cooking, much of this meal's preparation is done quickly at the last minute, though you should certainly start marinating the sliced beef for the stir-fry before guests arrive. The gelatin dessert, of course, requires several hours' advance preparation; feel free to substitute your favorite commercial flavored gelatin dessert.

VELVET CHICKEN–SWEET CORN SOUP

The "velvet" refers to the luxurious, slightly creamy quality of this classic Chinese soup, as well as to the bits of ground chicken breast that float in it along with the corn.

> 1½ quarts chicken broth
> ¼ pound ground chicken breast
> 1 tablespoon cornstarch
> ¼ cup milk
> 2 teaspoons light soy sauce
> 2 eggs
> 1 cup drained canned sweet corn
> 1 tablespoon finely chopped fresh
>   parsley
> 1 scallion, very thinly sliced

Set aside ¼ cup of the chicken broth. In a medium saucepan over moderate heat, bring the remaining chicken broth to a boil; reduce the heat to a bare simmer. Crumble in the chicken breast, breaking it into small pieces.

In a small bowl, dissolve the cornstarch in the milk; stir in the soy sauce. In a separate bowl, lightly beat the eggs and whisk in the reserved broth.

Stir the cornstarch mixture into the soup. As soon as it begins to thicken, add the egg mixture and corn and stir vigorously to break up the egg into thin wisps as it cooks. Serve immediately, garnished with parsley and scallion.

CHINESE-STYLE GINGER-BEEF AND VEGETABLE STIR-FRY WITH LO MEIN

A pound of lean beefsteak goes a long way when stir-fried with vegetables and tossed with Chinese noodles.

¼ cup light soy sauce
2 tablespoons rice vinegar or dry
   sherry
1½ tablespoons cornstarch
1 tablespoon grated fresh ginger root
1 pound good-quality lean beefsteak,
   thinly sliced
¾ pound uncooked Chinese egg
   noodles
¼ cup peanut or corn oil
1 medium clove garlic, finely
   chopped
1 medium red bell pepper, quartered,
   stemmed, seeded, and cut crosswise
   into ¼-inch-wide strips

1 medium carrot, cut diagonally into
   ¼-inch-thick slices
1 medium onion, thinly sliced
½ cup drained canned sliced water
   chestnuts
2 ounces small snow peas, trimmed
1 cup beef broth
3 tablespoons finely chopped fresh
   cilantro

In a mixing bowl, stir together the soy sauce and vinegar or sherry. Dissolve ½ tablespoon of the cornstarch in the mixture, then stir in the ginger and add the beef, mixing thoroughly to coat the slices. Marinate at room temperature 15 to 30 minutes.

Bring a large pot of salted water to a boil and add the noodles; cook until al dente, following package directions.

In a large wok or skillet, heat 2 tablespoons of the oil over moderate to high heat. Add the garlic and vegetables and stir-fry until the vegetables are tender-crisp, 2 to 3 minutes. Empty the vegetables into a mixing bowl.

Heat the remaining oil in the skillet. Remove the beef slices from their marinade, reserving the marinade, and stir-fry until they begin to brown, about 5 minutes. Return the vegetables to the wok with the marinade and ¾ cup of the broth. Dissolve the remaining cornstarch in the remaining broth and, as soon as the liquid in the wok begins to simmer, stir in the cornstarch mixture. Continue simmering just until the liquid thickens to thin coating consistency, about 1 minute. Then add the cooked and drained noodles and toss well to mix them with the other ingredients and coat them with sauce. Serve immediately, garnished with cilantro.

MANDARIN GELATIN

Beating egg whites into the hot gelatin mixture, then straining them out through cheesecloth, produces a dessert of sparkling clarity.

1½ cups cold water
1¼ cups sugar
2 tablespoons plus 2 teaspoons
    unflavored powdered gelatin
2 tablespoons fresh lemon juice,
    strained through a double
    thickness of cheesecloth

2 large egg whites, lightly beaten
1¼ cups fresh mandarin, tangerine,
    or orange juice, strained through a
    double thickness of cheesecloth
½ cup well-drained canned
    mandarin segments, chilled
Fresh mint sprigs, for garnish

In a heavy saucepan, stir together the water, sugar, gelatin, and lemon juice. Continue stirring over low heat until the sugar and gelatin dissolve; raise the heat slightly and continue cooking until the liquid barely begins to simmer. Remove the pan from the heat, cover, and let stand for about 30 minutes.

With a wire whisk, rapidly stir the egg whites into the gelatin mixture; then return the pan to low heat and whisk gently until a foam of egg whites forms on the surface. Pour the contents of the pan through a strainer lined with a double thickness of cheesecloth into a glass serving bowl.

Stir in the mandarin juice. Cover with plastic wrap and refrigerate until firmly set, 3 to 4 hours. To serve, scoop into individual chilled serving bowls and garnish with mandarin segments and mint sprigs.

6

CASUAL OCCASIONS

....

ANY OLD SPECIAL NIGHT

Serves 4

Roasted Pepper Salad
Pasta with Peas, Prosciutto, and Garlic Cream
Chianti-Raspberry Granita

Any night of the week can be special with a pasta menu composed of luxurious dishes easily prepared from widely available ingredients—some bell peppers, cream, peas, ham, an ordinary bottle of red wine, and some berries. To emphasize the meal's basic roots, serve it on your everyday dishware. Pour a crisp or medium-bodied white wine with the first and main courses.

Ideally, the granita should be prepared the day before, though you could scrape it together a few hours in advance; if time is short, substitute a fresh fruit sorbet. You can also roast the peppers from several hours to a day ahead, leaving them to marinate in the refrigerator until serving time.

ROASTED PEPPER SALAD

A motley profusion of roasted bell pepper strips enlivens this simple toss of greens.

*1 green bell pepper, roasted, peeled,
stemmed, and seeded (page 8),
torn into thin strips, juices
reserved*
*1 red bell pepper, roasted, peeled,
stemmed, and seeded (page 8),
torn into thin strips, juices
reserved*
*1 yellow bell pepper, roasted, peeled,
stemmed, and seeded (page 8),
torn into thin strips, juices
reserved*
*Balsamic Vinaigrette or Lemon
Vinaigrette (pages 7–8)*
*6 cups mixed salad greens (butter
lettuce, red leaf lettuce, radicchio,
romaine, etc.), washed and chilled*
*2 tablespoons finely chopped fresh
chives*
*2 tablespoons finely chopped fresh
parsley*

In a mixing bowl, toss the peppers and their juices with the vinaigrette. Cover with plastic wrap and refrigerate at least 30 minutes or until serving time.

Just before serving, tear the salad greens into bite-sized pieces and put them in a large salad bowl. Lift the pepper strips out of the dressing and add them to the greens. Add the chives and parsley and toss with just enough of the dressing to coat the leaves generously. Serve immediately.

PASTA WITH PEAS, PROSCIUTTO, AND GARLIC CREAM

If you can't find prosciutto, substitute any good-quality, fairly salty cured ham. Serve over medium ribbons such as fettucine or medium shapes such as shells or bow ties.

½ cup white wine vinegar
½ teaspoon salt
1 large clove garlic, coarsely chopped
3 cups heavy cream
¾ pound uncooked pasta
1½ pounds peas, shelled and parboiled for 2 to 3 minutes, until barely tender
¼ pound thinly sliced prosciutto, cut into strips about ¼-inch wide and 1-inch long
½ cup grated Parmesan
Freshly ground black pepper
2 tablespoons finely chopped fresh chives

Put the vinegar, salt, and garlic in a medium saucepan and bring to a boil over moderate to high heat; boil briskly until the vinegar reduces by half, about 5 minutes.

Add the cream and bring to a full boil. Reduce the heat slightly and simmer until the sauce reduces by about half to a thick coating consistency, about 20 minutes.

Meanwhile, bring a large pot of salted water to a boil and add the pasta; cook until al dente, following package directions.

Pour the sauce through a sieve to remove the garlic pieces. Return it to the pan over low to moderate heat and add the peas and prosciutto; sprinkle and stir in the Parmesan. When the sauce is hot and bubbly, pour over the cooked and drained pasta, season to taste with black pepper, and garnish with chives.

CHIANTI-RASPBERRY GRANITA

The combination of deep ruby color and icy, crystalline texture is especially appealing. Prepare this dessert a day in advance; take it out of the freezer about 30 minutes before serving to soften to a thick, slushy consistency, or put the solid-frozen mixture in a food processor and pulse the machine until the desired consistency is achieved.

> 1 pint fresh or defrosted frozen
>   raspberries
> ¾ cup water
> ¾ cup superfine sugar
> 2 cups Chianti or other light- to
>   medium-bodied dry red wine
> ¼ cup fresh lemon juice
> Fresh mint sprigs, for garnish

Reserve a small handful of whole raspberries and, in a food processor, puree the remainder. With a wooden spoon, press the puree through a fine sieve; reserve the puree and discard the seeds.

In a saucepan, stir together the water and sugar. Bring to a boil over moderate heat, stirring to dissolve the sugar. Boil for 1 minute, pour into a bowl, and let cool to room temperature.

Stir in the Chianti, lemon juice, and raspberry puree and pour into a shallow metal pan or pans. Transfer the pan to the freezer. Every 30 minutes to 1 hour, stir the mixture with a fork, scraping ice crystals from the side toward the center, continuing until it forms a thick, scoopable slush.

Scoop the granita into chilled dishes and garnish with whole raspberries and mint sprigs.

DINNER FOR OLD FRIENDS

Serves 4

Asparagus Vinaigrette (page 56)
Spaghetti with Lamb Bolognese
Garlic-Herb Loaf (page 30)
Lemon-Ginger Mousse (page 138)

Treat old friends to a meal that's comfortingly homey yet out of the ordinary by dishing up a pasta sauce that looks like a trattoria standard but is made with ground lamb instead of beef. Fresh asparagus to start, a crusty and fragrant loaf of bread, and a light, refreshing dessert complete a memorable meal. Break out some attractive tableware to underscore the welcome, and pour a good Italian red wine.

The pasta sauce may be made up to a day ahead of time and kept in the refrigerator; to allow for reheating, just cook until it is slightly more liquid than serving consistency. The mousse requires several hours of advance preparation and may be made the day before as well. You can also cook the asparagus and refrigerate it in its dressing several hours before mealtime.

SPAGHETTI WITH LAMB BOLOGNESE

If your butcher's display case doesn't include ground lamb, select lean stewing lamb and have it ground to order.

> 2 tablespoons olive oil
> 2 medium cloves garlic, finely
>   chopped
> 1 medium onion, finely chopped
> ¾ pound ground lean lamb
> 1 28-ounce can crushed tomatoes
> 2 tablespoons tomato paste
> 2 tablespoons fresh lemon juice
> 1 tablespoon dried basil
> 1 tablespoon dried oregano
> ½ tablespoon sugar
> ½ teaspoon salt
> ½ teaspoon black pepper
> 1 bay leaf
> ¾ pound uncooked pasta
> 2 tablespoons finely chopped fresh
>   parsley

In a large skillet or saucepan, heat the olive oil over moderate heat. Add the garlic and onion and sauté until tender, 2 to 3 minutes.

Add the lamb and raise the heat slightly. Sauté until it has lost all its pink color and left a brown glaze on the pan, about 10 minutes.

Add the tomatoes, stirring and scraping to deglaze the pan deposits. Stir in the tomato paste, lemon juice, basil, oregano, sugar, salt, pepper, and bay leaf. Simmer gently until the sauce is thick but still slightly liquid, 20 to 25 minutes.

While the sauce is simmering, bring a large pot of salted water to a boil and add the pasta; cook until al dente, following package directions.

Spoon the sauce over the cooked and drained pasta and garnish with parsley.

FIRESIDE SUPPER

Serves 4

Smoked Trout Pâté with Watercress
Baked Macaroni and Cheese with Bacon
Frozen Tangerine Sherbet

When the weather is cold, dinner by the fireside is a special pleasure. This menu of comfort foods enhances the pleasure even more, from a smooth seafood pâté that can be served and eaten communally, through a favorite old-time pasta dish, to a frozen dessert meant to brighten the palate at dinner's end. Use your most informal dishes, and feel free to even set them on the floor instead of on a table. Serve red wine, beer, or mulled cider.

Make the first and last courses up to several hours or even a day ahead of time. The pasta, too, can be assembled in its baking dish, covered with foil, and held in the refrigerator—ready to put into the oven just before you sit down to eat the appetizer.

SMOKED TROUT PATE WITH WATERCRESS

You'll find smoked trout in well-stocked deli cases. Serve with thinly sliced black bread, thinly sliced white toast, or crackers.

> ¾ pound smoked trout, skinned,
>   filleted, and flaked
> ¾ cup heavy cream
> 2 tablespoons grated horseradish
> 1 tablespoon fresh lemon juice
> 1 tablespoon grated orange zest
> ¼ teaspoon salt
> ¼ teaspoon white pepper
> ½ cup drained ricotta cheese
> ¾ cup coarsely chopped watercress
>   leaves
> Fresh watercress sprigs, for garnish
> 1 lemon, cut into wedges

Put the trout, cream, horseradish, lemon juice, orange zest, salt, and pepper in a food processor and process until smoothly blended, stopping once or twice to scrape down the bowl. Add the ricotta and pulse until blended in.

Remove the mixture to a mixing bowl and fold in the chopped watercress. Pack into a bowl, cover with plastic wrap, and refrigerate for at least 1 hour.

To serve, arrange watercress sprigs on individual serving plates. Generously scoop the mixture into the center of each plate and serve with lemon wedges.

BAKED MACARONI AND CHEESE WITH BACON

If you like, spice up the cheese sauce with a dash of hot pepper sauce or a teaspoon of creamy mustard. Shredded ham may be substituted for the bacon.

8 rashers lean smoked bacon
¾ pound uncooked elbow macaroni
3 cups milk
2 tablespoons cornstarch
1½ pounds sharp cheddar, coarsely
  shredded
½ cup grated Parmesan

Preheat the oven to 350°F.

In a heavy skillet, fry the bacon until crisp. Drain on paper towels and set aside.

Meanwhile, bring a large pot of salted water to a boil and add the macaroni; cook until al dente, following package directions.

While the macaroni is cooking, prepare the sauce. In a bowl or cup, stir ¼ cup of the milk with the cornstarch until the cornstarch dissolves. In a medium saucepan, bring the remaining milk almost to a boil; reduce the heat to a simmer and stir in the cornstarch mixture. Simmer until the milk thickens, 1 to 2 minutes, then stir in all but a generous handful of the cheddar and all of the Parmesan.

As soon as the cheese melts, add the cooked and drained macaroni, crumble in the bacon, and stir well. Transfer to a buttered baking dish and sprinkle the remaining cheddar on top. Bake until the sauce is bubbly and the cheese is browned, about 45 minutes.

FROZEN TANGERINE SHERBET

A touch of beaten egg white added during freezing gives this iced dessert the smoothness associated with a sherbet. Use fresh orange juice, if you like, in place of the tangerine juice.

> *2 cups strained freshly squeezed*
> * tangerine juice*
> *½ cup strained freshly squeezed*
> * lemon juice*
> *½ cup sugar*
> *1 tablespoon grated tangerine zest*
> *1 egg white*

In a heavy saucepan, stir together the tangerine and lemon juices and the sugar; bring to a boil over moderate heat, stirring continuously to dissolve the sugar. Stir in the tangerine zest, remove from the heat, and let the mixture cool to room temperature.

Transfer the mixture to a commercial ice-cream maker and start to freeze following manufacturer's directions. Meanwhile, beat the egg white until it just begins to turn frothy and opaque. As soon as the sherbet mixture begins to turn thick and slushy, stop the machine and add the egg white; then continue processing until completely frozen.

CUCINA DI CASSA

Serves 4

Bruschetta
Classic Potato Gnocchi with Butter and Sage
Fresh Pineapple with Vanilla Mascarpone

The title translates as "home cooking"—apt words, indeed, for a menu of simple, satisfying, heartwarming dishes. Put the food out on humble, homestyle crockery—the kind you'd use to serve a meal right in the kitchen. Offer white or light red wine, or beer.

You can mix and shape the gnocchi up to several hours or a day ahead of time, keeping them in a single covered layer on a baking sheet in the refrigerator. The tomato topping for the first course may also be made several hours in advance and refrigerated, as can the pineapple's mascarpone topping.

BRUSCHETTA

This simple peasant-style appetizer has become the chic dish with which to start a meal in trendy trattorias. It's at its best when vine-ripened tomatoes are in season.

3 tablespoons balsamic vinegar
½ teaspoon salt
½ teaspoon white pepper
½ cup olive oil
6 firm ripe Roma tomatoes, cored, halved, seeded, and coarsely chopped
1 tablespoon finely chopped fresh chives
1 tablespoon finely chopped fresh parsley
2 cloves garlic, pressed through a garlic press
12 ½-inch-thick slices Italian-style sourdough bread

Preheat the broiler or grill until very hot.

In a mixing bowl, stir together the vinegar, salt, and pepper until the salt dissolves. Stir in half the olive oil and toss with the tomatoes, chives, parsley, and half the garlic. Set aside.

In a small bowl, stir together the remaining oil and garlic. Brush the mixture on both sides of each bread slice and broil or grill until golden brown, 2 to 3 minutes per side.

Heap the tomato mixture on each bread slice and serve immediately.

CLASSIC POTATO GNOCCHI WITH BUTTER AND SAGE

Little dumplinglike potato gnocchi are among the most humble and satisfying pasta dishes—and surprisingly easy to make. The fresh herbs added to the mixture here contribute extra color and flavor to the dish. Don't use a food processor to make the gnocchi mixture: the speed of its blades will make the dumplings gummy.

6 medium baking potatoes, peeled
  and cut into 2-inch chunks
1 cup (2 sticks) unsalted butter,
  softened
1 teaspoon salt
1 teaspoon white pepper
1 egg, lightly beaten
1 egg yolk, lightly beaten

¼ cup grated Parmesan
2 tablespoons finely chopped fresh
  chives
2 tablespoons finely chopped fresh
  parsley
½–¾ cup all-purpose flour
2 tablespoons finely chopped fresh
  sage leaves

Put the potatoes in a large saucepan of salted water, bring to a boil, and cook until tender, 15 to 20 minutes. Drain well.

In a mixing bowl, mash the potatoes with a potato masher. Let them cool about 30 minutes.

With the masher, blend in 2 tablespoons of the butter, along with the salt and pepper. Then mash in the egg, egg yolk, Parmesan, chives, and parsley until thoroughly blended. Gradually blend in enough of the flour to form a smooth, fairly dry but still soft dough.

On a floured work surface, roll out the dough into ropes ¾ to 1 inch in diameter. With a sharp knife, cut the ropes into ¾- to 1-inch pieces.

Bring a large saucepan of salted water to a boil, then reduce the heat to a bare simmer. Add the gnocchi, in batches if necessary to prevent overcrowding, and simmer until they are cooked through and rise to the surface, about 12 minutes; drain on paper towels.

When the gnocchi are almost done, melt the remaining butter in a large skillet over moderate heat. Add the sage leaves and sauté for about 1 minute. Add the gnocchi to the skillet and toss gently. Serve immediately.

FRESH PINEAPPLE WITH VANILLA MASCARPONE

Seek out mascarpone, the slightly tangy, pourable double-cream cheese from northern Italy's Lombard region; it's sold in cartons in gourmet stores and Italian delis. Substitute crème fraîche or lightly whipped heavy cream.

> 1 cup mascarpone, chilled
> 2 teaspoons confectioner's sugar
> ½ teaspoon vanilla extract
> 1 large ripe pineapple, peeled, cored,
>   and cut into ½-inch-thick slices
> Fresh mint sprigs, for garnish

In a mixing bowl, use a wire whisk to stir together the mascarpone, sugar, and vanilla. Cover with plastic wrap and refrigerate until serving time.

Arrange the pineapple slices on individual serving plates and drizzle with the mascarpone. Garnish with mint.

IMPROMPTU BRUNCH

Serves 4

Melon and Port Wine
Smoked Salmon and Scrambled Egg Pasta
Assorted Fruit Gellati and Biscotti (page 20)

Pasta for brunch? You'll answer a resounding "Yes!" once you try the satisfying main-course egg-and-pasta dish in this menu. To match the elegant weekend morning mood, the fruit appetizer gains color and flavor from a brief marination in sweet port wine; dessert is a refreshing array of gellati. Serve the meal on china with a bright floral pattern. For a very special occasion, pour a medium-dry sparkling wine with the meal; otherwise, freshly brewed coffee or tea will do just fine.

The melon starter and the dessert may be made well in advance of the meal, leaving only the pasta to be prepared just minutes before it is served.

MELON AND PORT WINE

Sweet, ruby-red port contributes beautiful color to cantaloupe, as well as complementing its spicy perfume. If you like, toss a few fine strips of prosciutto with the melon just before serving.

> 1 large cantaloupe, halved and
>   seeded
> ½ cup port wine
> 2 tablespoons confectioner's sugar
> 1 tablespoon grated lemon zest
> Fresh mint sprigs, for garnish

With a melon baller, scoop out neat balls of cantaloupe and put them in a mixing bowl. Add the port, sugar, and lemon zest and toss well. Cover with plastic wrap and refrigerate for 1 to 3 hours, stirring occasionally.

To serve, spoon the cantaloupe and liquid into individual chilled serving dishes. Garnish with mint.

SMOKED SALMON AND SCRAMBLED EGG PASTA

Though the combination may sound a bit odd at first, it makes one of the most satisfying pasta dishes imaginable. Be sure to use lean smoked salmon rather than lox, which is too rich and fatty for this recipe.

¾ pound uncooked pasta
8 eggs
½ cup grated Parmesan
¼ cup heavy cream
½ teaspoon salt
½ teaspoon freshly ground black
    pepper
¼ cup (½ stick) unsalted butter
¾ pound thinly sliced smoked
    salmon, cut into ½- by 1-inch
    pieces
2 tablespoons finely chopped fresh
    chives
2 tablespoons finely chopped fresh
    parsley

Bring a large saucepan of salted water to a boil; add the pasta and cook until al dente, following package directions.

Just before the pasta is done, lightly beat the eggs in a mixing bowl. Beat in the Parmesan, cream, salt, and pepper.

In a large skillet, melt the butter over low to moderate heat. Add the cooked and drained pasta and pour the egg mixture over it. Cook, stirring and tossing slowly but continuously, until the egg begins to curdle and coat the pasta. Add the salmon, chives, and parsley and continue to stir and toss just until the eggs are cooked but still creamy. Transfer to individual serving plates or shallow pasta bowls and serve immediately.

OLD-TIME ITALIAN DINNER

Serves 4

Chopped Salad (page 34)
Spaghetti and Meatballs Napolitano
Tiramisu with Amaretti (page 70)

When I was a kid, before there was even a pizzeria in my neighborhood, an Italian dinner meant spaghetti and meatballs. That old-time pasta dish is joined here by a classic appetizer salad and a dessert that, though relatively new in popularity, is a longstanding favorite in its country of origin. Serve on white plates or other traditional Italian restaurant tableware, and don't forget the checked tablecloth and napkins. Pour a Chianti or other brisk red wine.

You can make the dessert several hours or more ahead of time. The salad and pasta, however, are really at their best if prepared just before serving.

SPAGHETTI AND MEATBALLS NAPOLITANO

The soft bread crumbs and generous amount of egg contribute a light, moist consistency to the herbed meatballs, which simmer to doneness in a light tomato sauce. Though spaghetti is the traditional choice, any medium strands or ribbons will do.

½ pound lean ground beef
½ pound lean ground pork
3 eggs, lightly beaten
2 medium cloves garlic, pressed
    through a garlic press
1 small onion, finely chopped
1 cup fresh bread crumbs
2 tablespoons finely chopped fresh
    parsley

1 tablespoon dried basil
1 tablespoon dried oregano
1 teaspoon salt
½ teaspoon freshly ground black
    pepper
½ cup olive oil
Napolitano Sauce (page 125)
¾ pound uncooked pasta

In a mixing bowl, stir together the beef, pork, eggs, garlic, onion, bread crumbs, parsley, basil, oregano, salt, and pepper. In a large skillet, heat the olive oil over moderate to high heat. Moistening your hands with cold water, shape the mixture into 2-inch-diameter meatballs, carefully adding them to the skillet without overcrowding. Sauté them until evenly browned, about 5 minutes. Drain on paper towels and set aside.

Prepare the Napolitano Sauce in a large saucepan and, as soon as it is simmering, add the meatballs to cook through in the sauce.

Meanwhile, bring a large pot of salted water to a boil; add the pasta and cook until al dente, following package instructions.

Put the cooked and drained pasta in individual pasta bowls or a large serving bowl and spoon the sauce and meatballs on top.

SOMETHING FOR EVERYONE

Serves 4

Herb-Marinated Mushrooms
Spaghetti with Turkey Meatballs and Bell Pepper–Marinara Sauce
Vanilla Frozen Yogurt with Raspberry Swirl (page 48)

Sometimes, when a member of the family is strictly watching his or her diet, everyone else suffers at the dinner table. But that needn't be the case—as this everyday family-style meal demonstrates. A light but flavorful appetizer, followed by a main course and dessert featuring simple, healthy substitutions for higher-fat, higher-calorie ingredients, results in a meal that is guaranteed to please everyone. Serve it on your everyday dishes, of course, and pour a light- to medium-bodied white or light red wine.

Both the appetizer and the dessert are made well in advance, leaving only the meatballs and pasta sauce to start cooking 30 to 45 minutes before mealtime.

HERB-MARINATED MUSHROOMS

Lightly sautéing the mushrooms in a little olive oil before they are marinated helps emphasize their natural meatlike flavor.

¼ cup olive oil
½ pound small cultivated
    mushrooms
2 tablespoons fresh lemon juice
½ teaspoon sugar
¼ teaspoon salt
¼ teaspoon white pepper
1 tablespoon finely chopped fresh
    chives
1 tablespoon finely chopped fresh
    dill weed
1 tablespoon finely chopped fresh
    parsley
12 butter lettuce leaves
Fresh parsley or dill sprigs, for
    garnish

In a large skillet, heat 1 tablespoon of the olive oil over moderate to high heat. Add the mushrooms and sauté just until they begin to darken in color, 2 to 3 minutes. Remove from the heat and transfer to a mixing bowl.

In another bowl, stir together the lemon juice, sugar, salt, and pepper until the sugar and salt dissolve. Stir in the remaining oil, then the herbs. Pour over the mushrooms, toss well, cover with plastic wrap, and marinate in the refrigerator overnight, turning the mushrooms 2 or 3 times.

Before serving, arrange the lettuce leaves on individual serving plates. With a slotted spoon, remove the mushrooms from the marinade and place in the center of each plate. Garnish with parsley or dill sprigs.

SPAGHETTI WITH TURKEY MEATBALLS
AND BELL PEPPER–MARINARA SAUCE

Here, turkey replaces beef in these surprisingly satisfying and full-flavored meatballs, and bell peppers add complementary color, texture, and flavor to the sauce. Other medium strands or ribbons may be substituted for spaghetti.

1 pound ground turkey
2 egg whites, lightly beaten
1 egg, lightly beaten
1 medium clove garlic, pressed
  through a garlic press
1 small red onion, finely chopped
1 cup fresh bread crumbs
¼ cup finely chopped fresh parsley
1 tablespoon dried rosemary
¾ teaspoon salt
½ teaspoon white pepper
Bell Pepper–Marinara Sauce (pages
  136–137)
¾ pound uncooked pasta

Preheat the broiler.

In a mixing bowl, stir together the turkey, egg whites, egg, garlic, red onion, bread crumbs, parsley, rosemary, salt, and pepper. Moistening your hands with cold water, shape the mixture into 1- to 1½-inch-diameter meatballs, placing them on the broiler tray. Broil until evenly browned, turning them once, about 5 minutes per side.

Prepare the Bell Pepper–Marinara Sauce in a large saucepan and, as soon as it is simmering, add the meatballs to finish cooking in the sauce.

Meanwhile, bring a large pot of salted water to a boil; add the pasta and cook until al dente, following package instructions.

Put the cooked and drained pasta in individual pasta bowls or a large serving bowl and spoon the sauce and meatballs on top.

COME ON OVER FOR DINNER

Serves 4

Romaine and Gorgonzola Salad
Beef-and-Sausage Bolognese with Shells
Coconut Crème Brûlée with Fresh Berries

An everyday dinner invitation needn't mean an all-out assault on the kitchen. Here, a few simple touches make a casual occasion special: crumbled Italian blue cheese in a simple, crisp salad; a classic Bolognese sauce elaborated with the addition of fresh Italian sausage; and a favorite dessert prepared with relative ease and made extra special with coconut and a few berries. Trot out your best china and glassware to make the easy meal sparkle even more. Pour a robust red wine to complement the pasta sauce.

The sauce can, in fact, be made the day before; don't cook it quite as long, so it will still be slightly liquid when you start to reheat it. Crisp the salad greens an hour or so in advance so they're ready to tear and toss at serving time. And make and assemble the crème brûlées up to a day before, leaving the final sprinkling and caramelizing of the sugar until moments before you serve them.

ROMAINE AND GORGONZOLA SALAD

Feel free to substitute another form of domestic or imported blue-veined cheese for the Gorgonzola.

> *6 cups well-chilled romaine lettuce,*
> *   torn into bite-sized pieces*
> *6 ounces Gorgonzola, crumbled*
> *Balsamic Vinaigrette (page 7)*
> *2 tablespoons finely chopped fresh*
> *   chives*

Put the lettuce in a large salad bowl. Add the cheese and toss well with enough vinaigrette to coat. Transfer the salad to individual chilled serving plates and garnish with chives.

BEEF-AND-SAUSAGE BOLOGNESE WITH SHELLS

Use sweet or spicy Italian sausage—whichever you prefer. The chunky, flavorful sauce goes especially well with shells or other medium-sized shapes or tubes such as bow ties, ruote, or mostaccioli. You can also serve it over medium strands or ribbons.

2 tablespoons olive oil
3 medium cloves garlic, finely
   chopped
1 large onion, coarsely chopped
1 large green bell pepper, halved,
   stemmed, seeded, and coarsely
   chopped
½ pound lean ground beef
½ pound fresh Italian sausage,
   casings slit, peeled off, and
   discarded
½ cup dry red wine

1 16-ounce can crushed tomatoes
2 tablespoons tomato paste
2 teaspoons sugar
2 teaspoons dried basil
2 teaspoons dried oregano
1 teaspoon dried thyme
½ teaspoon salt
½ teaspoon freshly ground black
   pepper
¾ pound uncooked pasta
2 tablespoons coarsely chopped fresh
   parsley

In a large skillet or saucepan, heat the oil over moderate heat. Add the garlic, onion, and bell pepper; sauté until tender, 2 to 3 minutes.

Add the beef and sausage and raise the heat slightly. Sauté, breaking up the meat into coarse chunks with a wooden spoon, until it has lost all its pink color and left a brown glaze on the pan, about 10 minutes. Carefully pour off any excess fat from the pan.

Add the wine and stir and scrape to dissolve the pan deposits. Add the tomatoes, tomato paste, sugar, basil, oregano, thyme, salt, and pepper. Simmer until thick but still slightly liquid, 15 to 20 minutes.

Meanwhile, bring a large pot of salted water to a boil; add the pasta and cook until al dente, following package instructions.

Spoon the sauce over the cooked and drained pasta and garnish with parsley.

COCONUT CREME BRULEE WITH FRESH BERRIES

If you're not a fan of coconut, feel free to leave it out of the recipe.

1⅓ cups heavy cream
4 egg yolks
3 tablespoons granulated sugar
½ teaspoon cornstarch
¼ cup shredded coconut
¾ teaspoon pure vanilla extract
¾ cup fresh blackberries, blueberries,
    raspberries, or a mixture
6 tablespoons light brown sugar

In the top of a double boiler, heat the cream just until bubbles begin to form at the edge. Remove it from the heat.

In a mixing bowl, use a wire whisk to beat the eggs until smooth and light lemon-yellow in color. In a separate bowl or cup, stir together the granulated sugar and cornstarch; gradually sprinkle and whisk into the yolks. Then, whisking the yolks continuously, slowly pour in the hot cream.

Pour the mixture back into the top of the double boiler and, over gently simmering water, stir continuously until the mixture forms a custard thick enough to coat a spoon, about 15 minutes. Remove the pan from the heat and stir in the coconut and vanilla. Let the mixture cool to room temperature, stirring occasionally.

Put the berries in the bottoms of individual custard cups or soufflé molds. Pour the custard on top, not quite to the rim, and smooth the surface level. Cover with plastic wrap and refrigerate until serving time.

About 15 minutes before serving, preheat the broiler. Put the cups in a baking pan and add ice and water to come halfway up their sides. Evenly sprinkle the brown sugar over the custard in each cup.

Put the pan under the broiler and broil just until the sugar melts and begins to bubble, 2 to 3 minutes; watch carefully to prevent burning. Remove from the heat, let the custards stand about 5 minutes, and then serve.

BRACING TASTES

Serves 4

Bruschetta (page 162)
Pasta with Broccoli and Garlic-Herb Cheese
Lemon-Champagne Granita (page 54)

Pasta lovers are often hearty eaters. With that in mind, this menu offers first and main courses of strong, satisfying tastes redolent of garlic and fresh herbs, followed by a bracing, palate-cleansing dessert. Serve on simple white dishware to highlight the bright colors and simple shapes of the food. Pour a robust white or light red wine with the meal.

Apart from the dessert, which is easily prepared the night before, little advance preparation is necessary.

PASTA WITH BROCCOLI AND GARLIC-HERB CHEESE

The rich, aromatic commercial cream-cheese spread does wondrous things for ordinary broccoli in this quickly assembled pasta dish. Serve over medium to wide ribbons or medium shells or bow ties.

6 cups packed broccoli florets
¾ pound uncooked pasta
¾ cup (1½ sticks) unsalted butter,
   cut into pieces
1 pound garlic-herb triple-cream
   cheese (such as Boursin)
Freshly ground black pepper

Bring a large pot of salted water to a boil. Add the broccoli and parboil for about 30 seconds; remove with a slotted spoon, leaving the water boiling.

Add the pasta to the boiling water and cook until al dente, following package directions.

A few minutes before the pasta is done, melt the butter in a large skillet over moderate heat. Add the broccoli florets and toss in the butter until thoroughly coated and heated through, about 2 minutes.

With your fingers, quickly drop clumps of the cream cheese over the broccoli. Stir until the cheese begins to melt and coat the broccoli. Immediately pour the sauce over the cooked and drained pasta. Season generously to taste with black pepper.

7

PASTA FOR LUNCH

....

FAMILY WEEKEND LUNCH

Serves 4

Assorted Antipasti
Pasta e Fagioli Soup
Caesar Salad (page 84)
Home-Churned Vanilla-Anise Ice Cream

Weekend lunch is one of the most casual of meals—a time to relax together over an array of easily prepared, easy-to-serve foods. To that end, a robust pasta-and-bean soup and a generous salad form the centerpiece of this menu, augmented by an array of Italian deli purchases and homemade or store-bought ice cream. Use everyday dishes. White or light red wine, or beer, would go well with the two featured dishes.

If you're planning on making your own ice cream, prepare it up to a week ahead or the night before. The soup, too, may be made ahead of time up to the point at which the pasta is added; start reheating, and add the pasta and enough broth or water to make the soup slightly fluid, about 20 minutes before serving. Be sure to allow an hour for the salad greens to crisp, too.

ASSORTED ANTIPASTI

Visit your local Italian or gourmet delicatessen to purchase an array of ready-to-serve Italian antipasti. Serve with crusty Italian bread and unsalted butter. Some suggestions:

> ½–¾ pound thinly sliced salami, pepperoni, prosciutto, or other sausage or ham
>
> ½ pound thinly sliced provolone cheese
>
> ½ pound block Parmesan, to be cut into thin curls with a cheese shaver
>
> 1–1½ pints marinated vegetables
>
> ½ pint cured black or green olives
>
> ½ pint pepperoncini

Arrange your selections attractively on a large platter.

PASTA E FAGIOLI SOUP

Serve this robust peasant soup with crusty Italian bread.

½ cup dried borlotti or lima beans
2 tablespoons olive oil
1 medium onion, finely chopped
1 medium clove garlic, finely chopped
1 large carrot, coarsely chopped
6 cups beef broth
1 smoked ham hock
½ tablespoon dried basil
½ tablespoon dried oregano
1 bay leaf
½ pound dried small elbow macaroni
  or shells
Salt and freshly ground black pepper
2 tablespoons coarsely chopped fresh
  parsley
½ cup freshly grated Parmesan

In a mixing bowl, cover the beans with cold water and leave to soak for about 12 hours.

In a large saucepan, heat the olive oil over moderate heat. Add the onion, garlic, and carrot and sauté until the onion and garlic begin to brown, 3 to 5 minutes.

Add the broth, ham hock, basil, oregano, and bay leaf. Drain the beans and add them. Bring to a boil, reduce the heat to low and simmer very gently, partially covered, until the beans are tender, about 1½ hours.

Add the macaroni and cook, uncovered, until al dente, 8 to 10 minutes more. Remove the ham hock, cut the meat from the bone, finely chop the meat, and return to the pan. Season to taste with salt and pepper and ladle into warmed bowls. Garnish with parsley and pass the Parmesan for guests to serve themselves.

HOME-CHURNED VANILLA-ANISE ICE CREAM

A splash of the popular Italian liqueur adds a hint of licorice flavor to this rich vanilla ice cream. Feel free to substitute some other liqueur; peppermint is especially good.

> 1 pint half-and-half
> 2 tablespoons Sambuca liqueur
> 1 teaspoon pure vanilla extract
> 2 whole eggs
> 1 egg yolk
> ½ cup sugar

In a heavy saucepan over moderate heat, warm the half-and-half just until bubbles begin to appear at its edge. Remove the pan from the heat and stir in the Sambuca and vanilla.

In a mixing bowl, use a wire whisk or electric beater on slow speed to beat the eggs, egg yolk, and sugar until thick, frothy, and pale yellow in color, 2 to 3 minutes. Beating continuously, slowly pour the half-and-half into the egg-and-sugar mixture.

Return the mixture to the saucepan over very low heat and cook, stirring and scraping continuously, just until the mixture is thick enough to coat a spoon, 3 to 5 minutes. Remove the pan from the heat and set the pan inside a baking pan filled with ice and water. Continue stirring until the mixture cools to room temperature.

Process the mixture in an ice-cream maker, following manufacturer's instructions. Serve at once while still soft-frozen. Or harden in the freezer and let the ice cream sit at room temperature before scooping and serving.

A SUMMERTIME GATHERING OF FRIENDS

Serves 4

Peppered Fresh Figs and Prosciutto
Chicken-and-Chutney Pasta Salad
Assorted Fruit Gellati and Biscotti (page 20)

A warm-weather get-together calls for casual, refreshing foods such as the cool, mildly spicy pasta salad that forms the centerpiece of this menu. Use your most casual tableware—even opting for plastic or nice paper plates if you choose to serve the meal outside. Pour a brisk, young white wine or chilled beer.

The pasta salad can be made up to several hours ahead of time. Wrapping the figs in prosciutto is a quick last-minute operation that ensures the ripe, succulent fruit are enjoyed at their best.

PEPPERED FRESH FIGS AND PROSCIUTTO

When summer's fresh figs are in season, there's no better foil for their succulent, slightly astringent sweetness than thinly sliced, salty-sweet prosciutto.

> *8 ripe fresh figs*
> *3–4 ounces very thinly sliced*
> *prosciutto*
> *Freshly ground black pepper*
> *Fresh mint sprigs, for garnish*
> *1 large lemon, cut into wedges*

Just before serving, cut the figs lengthwise into quarters. Cut the prosciutto slices into strips about 1 inch wide and wrap a prosciutto strip around each fig quarter. Arrange on individual serving plates or on a platter and season generously to taste with black pepper. Garnish with mint sprigs and serve with lemon wedges for guests to squeeze over individual portions.

CHICKEN-AND-CHUTNEY PASTA SALAD

You can make this with either leftover chicken or precooked roasted chicken from the supermarket. Use small or medium pasta shells or other shapes such as bow ties, ruote, or fusilli.

¾ pound uncooked pasta
2 tablespoons orange juice
1 teaspoon curry powder
¾ cup mayonnaise
6 tablespoons bottled mixed-fruit chutney, fruit pieces finely chopped
2 cups coarsely chopped cooked chicken
1 stalk celery, thinly sliced

1 scallion, thinly sliced
1 crisp green apple, cored and coarsely chopped
½ cup shelled cashew halves
½ cup seedless golden or dark raisins
2 tablespoons finely chopped fresh cilantro
16 whole butter lettuce or radicchio leaves

Bring a large pot of salted water to a boil; add the pasta and cook until al dente, following package directions. Drain well and rinse with cold running water. Set aside.

In a small bowl, stir together the orange juice and curry powder until the powder is completely dissolved. Put the mayonnaise in a larger bowl and add the orange-curry mixture and the chutney.

In a mixing bowl, toss together the cooked and drained pasta with the remaining ingredients except the lettuce. Add the mayonnaise dressing and toss well. Cover with plastic wrap and refrigerate until serving time.

Arrange the lettuce or radicchio leaves on individual plates or a platter and mound the pasta salad in the center.

IMPROMPTU PICNIC

Serves 4

Crudités Platter with Ripe, Creamy Cheeses
Pasta Cobb Salad
Marinated Oranges with Cinnamon Syrup (page 77)

Fresh vegetables; a cool, flavorful pasta salad; and ripe, juicy fruits make this menu a refreshing choice for dining al fresco. Bring along whatever picnic ware is easiest to pack and carry. Pour chilled white wine or spritzers of wine and sparkling water.

Of necessity, picnics must be make-ahead meals. That is why this menu works so well for a portable outdoor lunch. The vegetables may be cut in advance, packed in an airtight plastic container, and chilled in the refrigerator. The oranges, too, are easily made in advance. Toss the pasta with a little of the dressing and pack it in its own container; transport the other salad ingredients in separate containers, ready to toss together with the pasta and dressing at the picnic site just before serving.

CRUDITES PLATTER WITH RIPE, CREAMY CHEESES

Crudités—the French term for raw vegetables served as an hors d'oeuvre or appetizer—make an attractive, appealing start to a warm-weather meal, especially when served alongside one or more full-cream cheeses whose rich tastes and textures complement the vegetables' fresh flavor and crispness.

Let your market's best produce be your guide to the platter's final contents. Some good choices are bell peppers of varied colors, cut into thin wedges; small to medium-sized zucchini, quartered lengthwise; whole medium-sized mushrooms; whole cherry tomatoes; Belgian endive, separated into individual spear-shaped leaves; small radicchio leaves; jicama, peeled and cut into sticks; whole small scallions; and, of course, good old carrot and celery sticks.

For the cheese, ripe Brie and Camembert, and Italian fontina, are good choices. You might also want to add a creamy fresh goat cheese or a garlic-herb cream cheese.

Let guests spread the cheeses directly onto pieces of vegetable. Serve crackers with the cheese as well.

PASTA COBB SALAD

Pasta adds another satisfying dimension to the classic salad. If you like, substitute chicken or baby shrimp for the turkey. Assemble and toss the salad just before serving. Use small- to medium-sized shells or other shapes.

¾ *pound uncooked pasta*
Balsamic Vinaigrette or Lemon
    Vinaigrette (pages 7–8)
1 tablespoon creamy Dijon-style
    mustard
2 cups chopped cooked turkey breast
8 slices streaky smoked bacon, fried
    crisp and coarsely crumbled
4 firm ripe Roma tomatoes,
    stemmed, seeded, and coarsely
    chopped
4 hard-boiled eggs, finely chopped
6 ounces blue cheese, crumbled
2 medium firm ripe Haas avocados,
    halved, pitted, peeled, and cut into
    ½-*inch chunks*
2 medium scallions, thinly sliced

Bring a large pot of salted water to a boil; add the pasta and cook until al dente, following package directions. Drain well and rinse with cold running water. Set aside.

In a mixing bowl, stir together the vinaigrette and the mustard.

In a salad bowl, toss the cooked and drained pasta with a small amount of the dressing—just enough to coat it lightly. Arrange the remaining ingredients in a decorative pattern on top of the pasta. At table, toss the salad with enough of the remaining dressing to coat all the ingredients.

FRESH AND FLAVORFUL

Serves 4

Simple Salad of Baby Greens (page 14)
Pasta with Roma Tomatoes and Fresh Mozzarella
Mocha Mousse (page 62)

Light, fresh first and main courses delight the palate in this simple midday menu, allowing the slight indulgence of a chocolate-and-coffee–flavored confection to conclude the meal. Serve on simple, plain-colored, or clear-glass dishware to show off the bright colors of the salad greens and tomatoes. Offer a light, crisp white wine or spritzers.

The mousse may be made several hours ahead of time or the night before. Both the salad and the pasta are quick last-minute preparations.

PASTA WITH ROMA TOMATOES
AND FRESH MOZZARELLA

Fresh mozzarella has a lightness of taste and texture that the usual packaged product can't match. If your gourmet market or Italian deli carries it, by all means include it in this simple recipe; if not, the packaged product will do fine. Serve over thin to medium strands or ribbons.

¾ pound uncooked pasta
¼ cup olive oil
2 large cloves garlic, finely chopped
1½ pounds firm ripe Roma tomatoes,
　　peeled and seeded (page 9), and
　　coarsely chopped
½ tablespoon dried oregano
1 teaspoon sugar
½ teaspoon salt
1 pound fresh mozzarella, well-
　　drained and cut into ½-inch cubes
¼ cup finely shredded fresh basil

Bring a large pot of salted water to a boil; add the pasta and cook until al dente, following package directions.

While the pasta is cooking, heat the oil in a large skillet over moderate heat. Add the garlic and sauté 30 seconds to 1 minute. Add the tomatoes, oregano, sugar, and salt and sauté until the tomatoes' juices just begin to thicken, about 5 minutes.

Add the mozzarella and continue sautéing just until the cheese begins to melt, 1 to 2 minutes more. Spoon over the cooked and drained pasta and garnish with basil.

CASUAL LUNCH

Serves 4

Fresh Fines Herbes–Tomato Salad
Carbonara with Prosciutto
Chocolate-Orange Sherbet

Informal though the food is, this menu plays a beguiling balancing act between light and rich—starting with a simple tomato salad, then moving on to one of the richest dishes in the pasta repertoire, and concluding with a dessert that combines both lightness and richness in every spoonful. Serve it on your most sparkling, elegant dishware, which will further highlight the food's utter simplicity. Pour a full-bodied white or light red wine.

You can make the sherbet up to a day ahead of time, but make sure that you remove it from the freezer about 30 minutes before serving to ensure it is soft enough to scoop. The salad and pasta are both easy last-minute preparations.

FRESH FINES HERBES–TOMATO SALAD

There's something especially appealing about the simplicity of vine-ripened tomatoes sliced and arranged on a plate, adorned only with flecks of fresh herb and a light drizzle of oil and vinegar. Out of season, Roma tomatoes are your best choice.

> *1½ pounds vine-ripened tomatoes*
> *1 tablespoon finely chopped fresh basil*
> *1 tablespoon finely chopped fresh chives*
> *1 tablespoon finely chopped fresh dill weed*
> *1 tablespoon finely chopped fresh parsley*
> *Balsamic vinegar*
> *Olive oil*
> *Salt and freshly ground black pepper*

Just before serving time, core the tomatoes and cut them into ¼- to ½-inch-thick slices. Arrange them in an attractive pattern on individual serving plates or a platter.

Toss together the herbs and scatter them over the tomatoes. Pass vinegar, oil, salt, and pepper for guests to sprinkle over the tomatoes to taste.

CARBONARA WITH PROSCIUTTO

The traditional "charcoal maker" pasta dish gains a hint of elegance by substituting prosciutto for the usual bacon. Serve over spaghetti or linguine.

> ¾ pound uncooked pasta
> ¼ cup (½ stick) unsalted butter
> 2 medium cloves garlic, finely
>   chopped
> ½ pound thinly sliced prosciutto, cut
>   into ¼-inch by 2-inch strips
> 6 egg yolks
> 1½ cups heavy cream
> 1½ cups grated Parmesan
> 1½ tablespoons finely chopped fresh
>   chives
> 1½ tablespoons finely chopped fresh
>   parsley
> Freshly ground black pepper

Bring a large pot of salted water to a boil; add the pasta and cook until al dente, following package directions.

When the pasta is almost done cooking, melt the butter in a large skillet over low to moderate heat. Add the garlic and sauté about 1 minute. Scatter in the prosciutto and sauté about 30 seconds more. Remove from the heat.

In a mixing bowl, beat the egg yolks, cream, and Parmesan until well blended.

As soon as the pasta is cooked and drained, add it to the skillet and return the pan to low heat. Add the yolk-cream mixture, chives, and parsley and toss the pasta in the skillet, seasoning to taste with pepper, until the sauce thickens and coats the strands, 2 to 3 minutes.

CHOCOLATE-ORANGE SHERBET

Lighter than an ice cream, this iced dessert counterbalances the richness of chocolate with the tang of fresh orange.

1½ cups unsweetened cocoa powder
1 cup sugar
Pinch of salt
1 cup plus 2 tablespoons lowfat milk
1¾ cups strained fresh orange juice
3 tablespoons grated orange zest
2 egg whites, at room temperature

In a heavy saucepan, stir together the cocoa powder, sugar, and salt. With a wooden spoon, slowly stir in the milk, breaking up any lumps that form. Stir in the orange juice.

Put the pan over moderate heat and bring the mixture to a boil, stirring continuously to dissolve the cocoa and sugar. Reduce the heat to low and simmer, stirring continuously, for about 5 minutes. Remove the pan from the heat.

Put the pan in a baking pan filled with ice and water and stir until the mixture has cooled to room temperature. Stir in the orange zest.

Transfer the mixture to a commercial ice-cream maker and start to freeze following manufacturer's directions. Meanwhile, beat the egg whites until they just begin to turn frothy and opaque. As soon as the sherbet mixture begins to turn thick and slushy, stop the machine and add the egg whites; then continue processing until completely frozen.

BISTRO FARE

Serves 4

Smoked Trout Pâté with Watercress (page 158)
Spaghetti Aglio e Olio
Chianti-Raspberry Granita (page 154)

This easy lunch brings to mind the kind of simple fare you might enjoy at a
well-loved local bistro: a cool, flavorful pâté to start; an exquisitely simple,
flavorful pasta dish; and a bracing iced dessert to chase away the garlic fumes.
Serve it on bistro-style tableware, of course, and offer a crisp white or slightly
chilled light red wine.

Prepare the granita the day before; the pâté can be made that far in
advance, too. But the pasta dish is a last-minute preparation—and an incredibly
easy one.

SPAGHETTI AGLIO E OLIO

Quickly made from just a handful of ingredients, this is one of the great pasta dishes—a dramatically simple marriage of garlic, olive oil, and spaghetti or other medium strands. Vary the amount of garlic according to personal taste.

> ¾ *pound uncooked pasta*
> ½ *cup olive oil*
> *2–4 medium cloves garlic, finely*
>   *chopped*
> *2 tablespoons finely chopped fresh*
>   *parsley*
> *Salt and freshly ground black pepper*

Bring a large pot of salted water to a boil; add the pasta and cook until al dente, following package directions.

When the pasta is almost done, heat the oil in a large skillet over moderate heat. Add the garlic and sauté just until it begins to turn golden, about 1 minute.

Pour the garlic and oil over the cooked and drained pasta. Add the parsley, salt and pepper to taste, and toss well. Serve immediately.

PASTA IN THE GARDEN

Serves 4

Chilled Tomato-Orange Soup
Garden-Style Tuna Salad with Fusilli
Coconut-Pineapple Custard

Even if you serve this menu indoors, you'll feel as if you're having lunch in the garden, so fresh, cool, and bright are its flavors and colors. Serve on sparkling white china, glassware, or floral-designed plates, and offer a crisp or slightly fruity white wine—or spritzers.

Everything can be made at least several hours ahead of time. The only work to do just before serving is garnishing the soup with the orange-zest sour cream, arranging the pasta salad on top of the greens, and taking the dessert custards out of the refrigerator.

CHILLED TOMATO-ORANGE SOUP

The splash of orange juice primarily serves to highlight the natural sweetness of the tomatoes in this refreshing, gazpacholike chilled soup. If sun-ripened tomatoes are not in season, substitute canned, drained Italian plum tomatoes.

1 cup good-quality fresh white bread
   crumbs
¼ cup olive oil
1 clove garlic, peeled
4 medium sun-ripened tomatoes,
   peeled and seeded (page 9),
   coarsely chopped
½ small red onion, peeled and
   coarsely chopped
2 cups tomato juice, chilled
¾ cup orange juice, chilled
¼ cup medium-dry sherry
Salt and white pepper
½ cup sour cream
2 tablespoons grated orange zest
1 tablespoon finely chopped fresh
   chives

In a food processor, puree the bread crumbs, olive oil, and garlic until they form a smooth paste, stopping 2 or 3 times to scrape down the bowl. Add the tomatoes and onion and process until smooth. Transfer to a bowl, cover with plastic wrap, and refrigerate for 2 to 3 hours.

With a wire whisk, stir in the tomato juice, orange juice, and sherry. Season to taste with salt and white pepper and refrigerate until serving time.

Before serving, lightly beat the sour cream with a small wire whisk to liquefy it slightly. Stir in the orange zest. Ladle the soup into chilled bowls and garnish with the sour cream and chives.

GARDEN-STYLE TUNA SALAD WITH FUSILLI

Spiral-shaped pasta adds a note of festivity to this fresh-tasting salad. Feel free to substitute any other medium-sized pasta shape.

¾ pound uncooked pasta
3 6-ounce cans oil- or water-packed tuna, drained and broken into ½- to 1-inch flakes
3 large firm ripe Roma tomatoes, cored, halved, seeded, and coarsely chopped
2 stalks celery, cut crosswise into ¼-inch slices
1 green bell pepper, roasted, peeled, stemmed, and seeded (page 8), torn into thin strips
¾ cup drained pitted black olives, cut into halves

¾ cup mayonnaise
3 tablespoons fresh lemon juice
2 tablespoons finely shredded fresh basil
2 tablespoons finely chopped fresh chives
2 tablespoons finely chopped fresh dill weed
2 tablespoons finely chopped fresh parsley
8 butter lettuce leaves
8 radicchio leaves

Bring a large pot of salted water to a boil; add the pasta and cook until al dente, following package directions. Drain well and rinse with cold running water.

In a mixing bowl, lightly toss together the cooked and drained pasta, tuna, tomatoes, celery, bell pepper, and olives. In a separate bowl, stir together the mayonnaise, lemon juice, and herbs. Add the dressing to the tuna-and-pasta mixture and toss well. Cover with plastic wrap and refrigerate until serving time.

Arrange the lettuce and radicchio leaves on individual plates or a platter and mound the pasta salad in the center.

COCONUT-PINEAPPLE CUSTARD

Coconut and pineapple add a hint of the tropics to this cool, smooth custard.

2 cups milk
½ cup shredded coconut
½ cup dried pineapple, finely
   chopped
2 egg yolks
1 egg
1½ tablespoons light brown sugar
Pinch of salt
1½ tablespoons unsalted butter

In a medium saucepan, bring the milk, coconut, and pineapple to a boil; reduce the heat and simmer gently for 15 minutes. Set aside.

In a mixing bowl, lightly beat together the egg yolks, egg, sugar, and salt.

Preheat the oven to 325°F. Bring a kettle of water to a boil.

Pour the milk mixture through a strainer lined with cheesecloth and press with a wooden spoon to extract all the liquid; discard the coconut and pineapple.

Whisking continuously, slowly pour about ¼ cup of the hot milk into the egg mixture. Then pour the eggs into the remaining milk and stir well.

Generously grease the inside of individual custard cups with the butter. Pour the custard mixture into the cups and put the cups in a shallow baking pan. Open the oven, pull out a shelf, and carefully place the pan on it; then pour boiling water into the baking pan to come halfway up the sides of the custard cups. Carefully slide the shelf into the oven.

Bake the custards until a small, sharp knife inserted into the center of one comes out clean, about 20 minutes. Carefully remove the pan from the oven and let the custards cool to room temperature. Then cover with plastic wrap and chill in the refrigerator at least 1 hour.

LIGHT MIDDAY MEAL

Serves 4

Apple, Ham, Swiss Cheese, and Endive Salad (page 98)
Orzo, Chicken, and Broccoli in Broth
Coconut Crème Brûlée with Fresh Berries (page 176)

This light yet satisfying meal features a main-course soup that gains extra body from rice-shaped pasta. Serve it on simple glass dishes or a springtime floral pattern. Pour a medium-bodied white wine.

Both the salad and the dessert may be made several hours ahead of time—though the crème brûlée requires a quick last-minute caramelization under the broiler. You can also precook the pasta and broccoli and keep them covered in the refrigerator, to be heated through in the broth just before serving. Start preheating the broiler when you finish cooking the main-course pasta soup.

ORZO, CHICKEN, AND BROCCOLI IN BROTH

Rice-shaped orzo adds satisfaction to a light, quickly prepared main-course soup. The slightly smaller, similarly shaped pasta sometimes known as risi may also be used, as may angel hair or vermicelli broken into 1-inch pieces before cooking.

> ½ *pound uncooked orzo*
> 1 *cup small broccoli florets*
> 6 *cups chicken broth*
> ¾ *pound boneless skinless chicken*
>   *breasts, trimmed and cut crosswise*
>   *into ¼-inch-wide strips*
> ½ *cup grated Parmesan*

Bring a large pot of salted water to a boil; add the pasta and cook until al dente, following package directions. Drain well and set aside.

At the same time, bring a saucepan of salted water to a boil and cook the broccoli until tender-crisp, 2 to 3 minutes. Drain well and set aside.

In the saucepan, bring the broth to a boil and reduce the heat to a bare simmer. Add the chicken strips and simmer until just cooked through, 2 to 3 minutes, skimming off any scum that rises to the surface. Add the pasta and broccoli and simmer until heated through, about 1 minute more.

Ladle the soup into heated bowls and pass Parmesan for guests to sprinkle into the soup to taste.

INDEX

· · · · · · · · · · · · · · · · ·